Your Career in Psychology: Industrial-Organizational Psychology

TARA L. KUTHER

Western Connecticut State University

THOMSON
——————————*—*— ™
WADSWORTH

Australia • Canada • Mexico • Singapore • Spain • United Kingdom • United States

Publisher: Vicki Knight
Acquisitions Editor: Marianne Taflinger
Editorial Assistant: Justin Courts
Marketing Manager: Chris Caldeira
Marketing Assistant: Laurel Anderson
Project Manager, Editorial Production:
    Megan E. Hansen

Print/Media Buyer: Lisa Claudeanos
Permissions Editor: Kiely Sexton
Copy Editor: Mary Anne Shahidi
Cover Designer: Roger Knox
Compositor: Brian May
Text and Cover Printer: Webcom

Printed in Canada
1 2 3 4 5 6 7 07 06 05 04

For more information about our products, contact us at:
Thomson Learning Academic Resource Center
1-800-423-0563
For permission to use material from this text, contact us by:
Phone: 1-800-730-2214
Fax: 1-800-730-2215

Web: http://www.thomsonrights.com

Library of Congress Control Number: 2004105952

ISBN 0-534-61778-6

Wadsworth/Thomson Learning
10 Davis Drive
Belmont, CA 94002-3098
USA

Asia
Thomson Learning
5 Shenton Way #01-01
UIC Building
Singapore 068808

Australia/New Zealand
Thomson Learning
102 Dodds Street
Southbank, Victoria 3006
Australia

Canada
Nelson
1120 Birchmount Road
Toronto, Ontario M1K 5G4
Canada

Europe/Middle East/Africa
Thomson Learning
High Holborn House
50/51 Bedford Row
London WC1R 4LR
United Kingdom

Latin America
Thomson Learning
Seneca, 53
Colonia Polanco
11560 Mexico D.F.
Mexico

Spain/Portugal
Paraninfo
Calle/Magallanes, 25
28015 Madrid, Spain

Tara L. Kuther, Ph.D. is Associate Professor of psychology at Western Connecticut State University, where she teaches courses in child, adolescent, and adult development. She values opportunities to conduct collaborative research with students and is active in the Council for Undergraduate Research as Psychology Councilor. Dr. Kuther is Chair of the Instructional Resource Award Task Force of the Office of Teaching Resources in Psychology (OTRP) of the Society for Teaching of Psychology, Division 2 of the American Psychological Association. She has taught both undergraduate and graduate courses at a wide range of institutions, including Lehman College (CUNY), Fordham University, and Teachers College, Columbia University. Her research examines risky behavior during adolescence and young adulthood, moral development, and ethics in research and teaching. She is the author of *The Psychology Major's Handbook,* and coauthor of *Careers in Psychology: Opportunities in a Changing World.* To learn more about Dr. Kuther's research, visit her website at *http://tarakuther.com*

Brief Contents

Contents

Chapter 3

Consultant   23

Chapter 4

Product Development and Environmental Design 41

Chapter 5

Academia and Research   51

Chapter 6

Is Industrial- Organizational Psychology or Human Factors For You?   67

References   77

PREFACE

Some of the fastest growing areas of psychology are collectively known as work psychology and represent the application of psychology withing business and industry, including the overlapping fields of industrial psychology, organizational psychology, and human factors psychology. Many students seek careers that merge their business and psychology interests, but don't know how to start or where to look for advice.

My goal in writing *Your Career in Psychology: Industrial-Organizational Psychology* is to introduce students to the variety of forms that careers in work psychology may take. Each chapter in *Your Career in Psychology: Industrial-Organizational Psychology* presents a career path, including an overview, advantages and disadvantages, and a profile of psychologist who has chosen that path. Consider this book a starting point for exploring careers in industrial, organizational, and human factors psychology. Discuss the career opportunities they find within these pages with your advisor and psychology professors.

Your Career in Psychology: Industrial-Organizational Psychology begins by discussing the nature of industrial, organizational, and human factors psychology and the diverse career paths available in this field. Chapter 2 explores careers in human resources departments for graduates with bachelor's and graduate degrees. Consulting careers, including management consulting, research consulting, and executive coaching, are presented in Chapter 3. Psychologist's roles in improving the design of equipment and products is discussed in Chapter 4. Chapter 5 explores research and academic careers of industrial, organizational, and human factors psychologists. The final chapter of *Your Career in Psychology: Industrial-Organizational Psychology* explores graduate training in work psychology and discusses what you can do now, as an undergraduate, to prepare and advance your career.

Acknowledgements

I am most appreciative of the constructive comments and helpful suggestions that I received from reviewers: [insert].

I thank Marianne Taflinger for taking this project under her wing, guiding it through the review and revision process, and sharing her expertise. Thanks to Vicki Knight for identifying the promise of this project and directing it to the appropriate channels to make it happen. Margarita Posada provided feedback and helpful suggestions that improved the quality of each chapter within this book. Finally, I thank my family: my parents, Philip and Irene Kuther, and my husband, Larry DeCarlo for their unwavering support through the years.

INTRODUCING WORK PSYCHOLOGY

CHAPTER GUIDE

There is no doubt that psychology, the study of human behavior, is an applied field—psychology helps us in our daily lives. It's also an extraordinarily diverse field, spanning from biology and lifespan development to cognition and perception, to mental health and pathology. Some of the fastest growing areas of psychology are collectively known as "work psychology" (Patterson, 2001), representing the application of psychology within business and industry, including the overlapping fields of industrial psychology, organizational psychology, and human factors psychology. About 6% of psychologists identify themselves as industrial, organizational, or work psychologists (Weiten, 2002), but many clinical and counseling psychologists are beginning to offer their services within business environments because of the decline in private practice opportunities associated with managed care (Somerville, 1998). Work psychologists interact with owners, managers, and employees of business and industry to select, train, and manage employees, design and market products, and organize work environments. Industrial and organizational psychologists apply psychological principles to the workplace, and human factors psychologists apply psychological principles in designing nearly everything that people encounter in their daily lives at work and at home (e.g., equipment, workspaces, computer software, and furniture).

FIELDS OF STUDY

Industrial Psychology

Industrial psychology, sometimes called personnel psychology, is the study of how individuals behave within work settings. Industrial psychologists practice psychology within the workplace and engage in a variety of activities, as described in the following sections.

Employee Selection and Placement. Appropriate selection and placement of employees promotes their overall job satisfaction, morale, and productivity. Industrial psychologists employ a scientific approach in developing and applying employee selection and placement methods that ensure that the right applicants are hired and employees' talents match their jobs. Industrial psychologists who specialize in employee selection and placement conduct extensive job analyses to determine the skills, abilities, and characteristics that are needed to be successful in a given job. They create, validate, and choose tests and interviews that are administered to job applicants to determine whether they should be hired and, if so, where they should be placed. Appropriate placement of employees entails identifying what jobs are most compatible with an employee's skills and interests, as assessed through questionnaires and interviews (Muchinsky, 2003). After placing employees, industrial psychologists conduct follow-up assessments to determine how well their selection and placement methods predict employee job performance—and refine their methods, when needed.

Employee Training and Development. The work of industrial psychologists doesn't end with selection and placement of employees; industrial psychologists are also involved in training employees and guiding them in their professional development. By conducting needs analyses, or large survey and interview-based assessments, industrial psychologists determine what skills and technical needs employees have or desire and develop training programs to impart those skills. They create assessment centers, or collections of assessment devices, questionnaires, vignettes or case study problems, and simulated work situations, to assess employees' problem-solving, communication, and other work-related skills and abilities (Tenopyr, 1997). Training needs may include assisting new employees during their transition to the workplace, updating current employees' technical skills, preparing employees for new responsibilities, and providing diversity training to retrain employees' attitudes, prejudices, and stereotypes (Scrader, 2001). Industrial psychologists also devise methods for evaluating the effectiveness of training programs and improve them based on those evaluations.

Employee Performance Appraisal. Industrial psychologists determine the criteria or standards by which employees will be evaluated. In other words, they determine how to define employee competence and success. Industrial psychologists choose, create, and validate methods for measuring employee effectiveness. They assess employees' abilities and performance, providing feedback and documentation about the quality and quantity of an employee's work to support pay increases and promotions (Aamodt, 2004; Muchinsky, 2003). Industrial psychologists train supervisors on how to perform these tasks to evaluate employee performance and communicate the results with sensitivity.

Promotion of Adherence to Laws and Participation in Litigation. Industrial psychologists understand legal issues related to the workplace (e.g., selecting, hiring, and promoting employees). They create policies and conduct regular training workshops to promote a positive work environment and to prevent harassment and other issues that contribute to a hostile work environment. Industrial psychologists are aware of laws regulating personnel procedures, help companies comply with laws, and help businesses and companies prepare for litigation activities in response to complaints from employees and former employees under the various federal, state, and local civil rights acts (Tenopyr, 1997). They may advise the company's attorneys and explain the science behind a company's hiring and promotion policies (i.e., the validity of the assessment tests and interviews). In court, an industrial psychologist must persuade judges and juries that his or her work (e.g., in selecting, placing, and evaluating an employee) was done correctly. As you might imagine, industrial psychologists who design employee selection and placement procedures must learn a great deal about civil rights laws and build compliance with the laws into their research and development efforts (Tenopyr, 1997). They must understand the legal context for personnel decisions and assist their employers in making personnel decisions that are legal. Companies seek advice from industrial psychologists on how to conduct layoffs with sensitivity while avoiding litigation from disgruntled former employees (Murray, 2002). Other industrial psychologists work as expert witnesses on behalf of either side of a labor or other form of personnel dispute, informing the court regarding personnel selection, placement, evaluation procedures, and other personnel-related activities.

Organizational Psychology

Industrial psychology and organizational psychology are closely related and overlapping fields whose distinctions are fuzzy because practitioners often share job descriptions and duties. Therefore, the two areas often are referred to jointly as industrial/organizational psychology. As we've discussed, industrial psychologists traditionally focus on the individual worker: selection, placement, training, and evaluation. The organizational psychologist works at the organizational level to understand how workers function in an organization and how the organization functions as a whole. The following activities are typically ascribed to organizational psychologists:

Promotion of Job Satisfaction and Quality of Work-Life. Organizational psychologists determine what factors contribute to a healthy and productive workforce. They examine job satisfaction within an organization and study factors that are associated with job satisfaction, such as employee turnover, absenteeism, age, pay, motivation, and attitudes toward the organization. Organizational psychologists develop and evaluate systems to promote job satisfaction by rewarding good performance and redesigning jobs to make them more challenging, meaningful, and satisfying to employees (Muchinsky, 2003). Promoting job satisfaction entails understanding workers' needs and creating incentives that build job commitment and loyalty. For example, organizational psychologists attempt to understand how Generation X workers are different from the generations that came before and how companies can tailor employee incentives to maximize their satisfaction (Cohen, 2002). They also study how employee services, such as office-based childcare and gym facilities, influence morale, job satisfaction, and productivity. Some organizational psychologists study the effects of job conditions like machine-paced work, shift work, and worker autonomy on worker health, as well as occupational stressors in specific occupations like nurses, police officers, coal miners, office workers, and occupational differences in stressors and stress-related disorders (Rosenstock, 1997).

Leadership Training.   Organizational psychologists study leadership: What makes a good leader? They identify characteristics of effective leaders and determine the types of leaders that are most effective in particular positions. They create individual and group training programs to improve the leadership and communication skills of supervisors and managers. In this way, organizational psychologists may act as executive coaches (Kilburg, 1996; Witherspoon & White, 1996).

Organizational Development.   Organizational psychologists help companies determine when changes are needed. They help organizations make changes, transition to new ways of managing things, and accept change. As Muchinsky (2003) explains, "Organizations grow and mature just as people do; thus, the field of organization development is directed toward facilitating the organizational growth process" (p. 6).

The organizational psychologist is a change agent who identifies problems, studies potential solutions, and makes recommendations (Tenopyr, 1997). An organizational psychologist might examine and refine business procedures such as develop a paperwork processing plan that is concise, consistent, and without unnecessary steps. Organizational psychologists help organizations to manage and resolve interpersonal problems. For example, an organizational psychologist might use conflict resolution skills to work out a solution for feuding departments or team members. Organizational psychologists examine the lines of authority or communication and redesign them when necessary.

Human Factors

Human factors psychology, sometimes called engineering psychology or ergonomics (especially in Europe), is the study of the interaction between humans and things—how people interact with their environments, and especially how they interact with machines (like computers). Human factors psychologists design work environments to optimize productivity, employee satisfaction, and safety, and limit stress, fatigue, and error. Some human factors psychologists specialize in human and computer interaction, or study how people interact with computers in order to improve computer applications and hardware designs. A human factors psychologist might study how to make Web sites more user friendly (Clay, 2000) or computer software more intuitive.

Others emphasize error prevention and management or the study of human error in order to predict and prevent errors through excellent design. In other words, human factors psychologists use their understanding of how people use products, and common mistakes that people are likely to make, in designing products to prevent error and misuse. For example, a human factors psychologist might work to reduce human error in medicine by improving the accessibility of software for recording patient information, streamlining reporting procedures, or adding cross-checks before surgeries or other medical procedures are conducted (Woods, 2002). Human factors psychologists can play a role in improving national security by deterring future terrorist threats directed toward air travel because they analyze and have tools to evaluate proposed changes in equipment, procedures, and regulations and study how they impact the efficiency of people operating them and the system as a whole (Hart, 2002).

Human factors psychologists attempt to design products, equipment, environments, and systems so that people are productive, satisfied, and safe (Wogalter & Rogers, 1998). They study work environments and determine how to modify environments to enhance productivity. For example, a human factors psychologist might adapt a work environment, including computer interfaces and other equipment, to compensate for the limitations and qualities of people to increase safety and reduce accidents. They study the effects of environmental factors such as light, noise, temperature, and work schedules (e.g., night shifts or compressed workweeks) on worker safety, productivity, and satisfaction (Muchinsky, 2003). In summary, human factors psychologists attempt to design products, equipment, environments, and systems so that people are productive, satisfied, and safe (Wogalter & Rogers, 1998).

As we've discussed, industrial, organizational, and even human factors psychologists often share job descriptions and duties. These psychologists are found in a variety of work settings, including businesses, consulting firms, universities, and government departments, as you'll see throughout this book.

SUGGESTED READINGS

Aamodt, M. G. (2004). *Applied industrial/organizational psychology.* Pacific Grove, CA: Wadsworth.

Blakeney, R., Broenen, R., Dyck, J., Frank, F., Glenn, D., Johnson, D., & Mayo, C. (2002). Implications of the results of a job analysis of I-O psychologists. *The Industrial-Organizational Psychologist.* Retrieved November 8, 2003 from http://www.siop.org/tip/backissues/TIPApr02/04blakeney.htm

Muchinsky, P. M. (2003). *Psychology applied to work.* Pacific Grove, CA: Wadsworth.

Nickerson, R. S. (Ed.). (1995). *Emerging needs and opportunities for human factors research.* Washington, DC: National Academy of Sciences. Available at: http://www.nap.edu/catalog/4940.html

Pond, S. B. (1999). Industrial-organizational psychology: The psychology of people working together. *Eye on Psi Chi, 3*(3), 34–37. Available at http://www.psichi.org/content/publications/eye/volume/vol_3/3_3/pond.asp

Tenopyr, M. L. (1997). Improving the workplace: Industrial/organizational psychology as a career. In R. Sternberg (Ed.), *Career paths in psychology: Where your degree can take you* (pp. 185–196). Washington, DC: American Psychological Association.

Wolgalter, M. S., & Rogers, W. A. (1998). Human factors/ergonomics: Using psychology to make a better and safer world. *Eye on Psi Chi, 3*(1), 23–26. Available at: http://www.psichi.org/content/publications/eye/volume/vol_3/3_1/wogalter.asp

WEB RESOURCES

Industrial Psychology
    http://www.a2zpsychology.com/psychology/industrial_psychology.htm

Ergonomics: The Science for Better Living and Working
    http://www.apa.org/ppo/issues/sergofact.html

Industrial/Organizational Psychology Links
    http://www.socialpsychology.org/io.htm

Society for Industrial and Organizational Psychology
    http://siop.org/

Human Factors and Ergonomics Society
    http://hfes.org/

What Is I/O Psychology?
    http://www.psy-lab.org/IOpsych.htm

PROFILE: BOBBIE RAYNES, M.S., PERSONNEL RESEARCH ASSOCIATES, INC. (SOURCE: AMMODT, 2004)

I work for a small human resources consulting company that offers public and private organizations a variety of services, including employee selection and performance evaluations instruments, salary and compensation studies, career assessment, employee and supervisory trainings, and conflict management through mediation or conflict management workshops. The part of my job I enjoy most is mediating workplace conflicts and teaching others how to better manage conflict. In today's business world, with all of the additional demands placed on employees and supervisors as a result of downsizing, reduced funding, and other organizational changes, conflict is inevitable. However, if these conflicts can be acknowledged and addressed quickly, it is much less likely that lawsuits will arise and more likely that employee morale and productivity will remain at an acceptable level. At least 90% of conflict situations that I have handled have been resolved through mediation.

Mediation can work for almost any type of conflict, including conflicts arising from employment issues (e.g., discrimination or sexual harassment) between employees and their supervisors, team members, and coworkers. However, for mediation to be most successful, certain criteria must be met, which include willingness from all parties to try the process, their desire to solve their problem without litigation, time to mediate (because mediation may take several days or weeks), and the perception that the mediator is impartial and the process will be confidential.

A good example of how important these criteria are involves one of my recent cases, which consisted of a team of 13 members who weren't getting along. I met individually with all 13 members and asked about their perceptions of the problem. All but one stated that one particular team member was the source of the problem. Apparently, this one member yelled a lot (they called him a "blowhard" who didn't take constructive criticism about his work performance well). Can you guess which team member didn't give this response? Of course, it was the alleged "blowhard" who was unable to see his role in the conflict. His answer instead was, "I don't know what the problem is. Everyone just seems mad at each other." After talking to him, I was sure he really didn't have a clue about the problems some of his behaviors were causing!

I asked each team member if they would like to try mediation, which meant that they all had to sit down at the same table and talk about what they felt was the source of the conflict and then brainstorm some ideas on how to resolve the problem. No one wanted to sit at the same table with the problem employee. Apparently, because this team member was a physically big man with a tendency to act out, other people were intimidated by him and felt he would retaliate in some way. For that reason, mediation wasn't the best strategy because parties weren't willing to meet to discuss their problems. Instead, we conducted an all day training session, which included role plays on how to communicate to each other about the perceptions of behavior. In this way, no one person was singled out, and during the role play we were able to talk about what were good communication behaviors and what kind of verbal or nonverbal communication could become a source of conflict. This gave the problem team member an opportunity to learn what behaviors he may have that were causing problems. I knew this training was successful when he spoke up after a role play and said, "Hey, I do that sometimes. I didn't realize how intimidating that can be." You could just see the relief on the other team members' faces when he made this announcement!

In another team situation involving five schoolteachers, there were two main sources of conflict. The first was that their new principal was not good at directing the teachers and explaining his expectations, so they weren't sure what they were supposed to be doing. The second source was the fact that the team had a fairly new teacher, fresh out of college, who had many new and innovative ideas she had learned in school and wanted to try out. The other four teachers had been there for many years and were comfortable with what they had been doing—they weren't real receptive to any type of change!

I often see this in mediations that involve employees and organizational change. Because most of us fear the unknown that change brings, it is easier not to try anything new. The key is to talk about what fears individuals have and then try to determine if those fears are real and, if they are, how to overcome those fears.

Mediation was very successful with this group because they were all friends and wanted to preserve their relationships, they were eager and willing to try the process, and there weren't any time constraints (which means we were able to have two or three different sessions in which they were able to air their concerns and then talk about how to resolve the conflict). Two basic solutions resulted from these mediation meetings. One was that the five teachers would ask the new principal to meet with them as a group to help them develop a set of clear expectations he had of them.

The second was that they would be more open to trying new ideas any of them might have. They asked that the next time the new teacher had an idea she wanted to try that she make sure she was able to clearly tell them how to go about implementing the new idea and what role each one of them would have in it.

Another good example of where mediation can be helpful is in employment issues, such as sexual harassment cases. Consider the role perceptions play in causing or resolving conflict. In this particular case, a woman perceived that one of her coworkers has harassing her by patting her on the rear end whenever she did a good job. It happened several times before she went to her supervisor and said she was being sexually harassed. The supervisor talked to both parties and asked if they would be willing to mediate this conflict. They were both willing, and I was called in as the mediator. I had the woman start the session by telling her coworker what she felt was the situation. After she talked, he simply hung his head and said, "I swear to you, I never meant anything by it. I guess I've always done that, and not just to women, but to my buddies. I never knew it bothered you. I grew up in a big family where we did that to each other all the time." In this situation, you can see that the woman's perception of being harassed was a misperception. However, just because it is a misperception doesn't mean it never should have been resolved. Probably 80% of my cases are based on misperceptions that, if not corrected, would have resulted in litigation. Once this woman was offered a safe environment in which to discuss her concerns, she was able to communicate her feelings and her desire that the behavior stop. Her coworker apologized to her, and she thanked him for being willing to listen to her and stop his behavior. She also acknowledged that it helped her to understand why he did that behavior. Last I heard, they have remained on good terms with each other.

Being a mediator has been challenging, but rewarding. Knowing that I have been instrumental in helping people preserve their relationships and resolve their differences has made all the hard work and hours I put into training for this position worthwhile.

I have been seeing more and more human resource specialists pursue training in this area so they can better manage their organization's day-to-day conflicts. If you are interested in this area, contact the National Institute for Dispute Resolution (NIDR), 1726 M Street, NW, Suite 500, Washington, DC, 20036-4502, (202) 466-4764, for general information.

CAREERS IN HUMAN RESOURCES

CHAPTER GUIDE

Students with interests in industrial and organizational psychology often seek careers in human resources. In organizational settings, personnel are viewed as resources; other resources include computers, software, equipment, and facilities. All organizations—large, small, private, public, profit, and nonprofit—must manage their human resources, their workers. Human resource departments, also known as personnel departments, oversee the people who work within organizations. Human resource departments help employers manage their employees by serving a variety of functions, including selection and placement, record keeping, wage and salary administration, training and development, benefits administration, and more. Human resources personnel work to attract the most qualified employees, match them to the jobs for which they are best suited, help them to succeed in their jobs, and ensure that the organization complies with labor laws (Society for Human Resource Management, n.d.). Human resource departments are found in all organizations: businesses, government, and private and nonprofit agencies. There are a variety of career paths within human resources departments depending on your education, interests, and experience.

HUMAN RESOURCE CAREERS

In very small organizations, most human resources tasks are handled by one, two, or a small handful of people. In large organizations, these tasks are managed by several subdepartments. Let's take a look at the tasks in which human resources personnel engage.

Employee Recruitment, Selection, and Placement

Human resource departments work to bring new employees into the organization. They recruit, interview, test, select, and place potential workers. They collect applications and resumes for jobs, assemble applicant files, perform background checks, interview applicants, administer preemployment assessments and tests, and place employees (Society for Human Resource Management, n.d.; Bureau of Labor Statistics, 2002). They identify the most qualified applicants and, usually, present them to the supervisor who will work with the new hire to make a final choice. If you work on employee recruitment, selection, and placement, you may orient new employees, educate employees about salary and benefits, and assess departmental needs for staffing. Common entry-level positions include interviewer, recruiter, employment representative, or EEO (equal employment opportunity) specialist. With advanced experience and/or education, you can take on a supervisory role in employee recruitment, selection, and placement as an employment and placement manager, HR analyst, or HR director.

Wage and Salary Administration

Wage and salary administrators, also known as compensation managers, assistant personnel directors, or at the entry-level, compensation specialists, are responsible for coordinating the wages and salaries in an organization (Traynor & McKenzie, 1994). Although it isn't possible to treat all employees the same, organizations must avoid inequities in wages. An effective wage and salary administration program is critical for keeping employees fairly compensated and maintaining an organization's competitiveness by attracting and retaining employees. Salary administrators compare an organization's pay rates with comparable firms to ensure that salaries are competitive. They may design systems to reward employees for outstanding performance (Bureau of Labor Statistics, 2002) and improve morale within an organization.

Job Analysis

Job analysis is a critical function of human resource departments. Job analysts, sometimes called position classifiers, prepare job descriptions by collecting and examining detailed information about job duties (Bureau of Labor Statistics, 2002). The job description explains the duties, training, and skills required of each position within an organization. Job analysis entails gathering information about a job through the use of interviews and surveys, and providing a job description or specification—the information provided describes a job within an organization, not a particular person.

Data provided by job analysts are useful to several human resources tasks. Job analysis is used in training and development of personnel, as job descriptions specify training needs for each position. Job descriptions are used by wage and salary administrators to identify appropriate compensation based on skill level, responsibilities, and education. Recruitment and selection procedures rely on job analysis to specify what job duties to include in advertisements of vacant positions, minimum education and experience requirements for screening applicants, interview questions, selection tests, and orientation materials for new hires. Job descriptions are also useful for performance review in developing goals and objectives, performance standards, evaluation criteria, and duties to be evaluated for a given position (HR-Guide.com, 2001).

Training and Development

The director of training, also known as manager of human resource development, manager of personnel training and development, or training coordinator, directs and coordinates training programs within an organization. The first step in developing an employee training system is to conduct a needs analysis to determine the types of training, if any, needed within an organization as well as whether training is an appropriate means of achieving an organization's goals. Human resource development, or training, helps workers to improve their job skills and become more efficient. Some organizations provide supervisors and managers with training in leadership and management techniques. Other common types of training include apprentice, supervisory, sales, recruiting, interviewing, and management. The director of training must consult with managers to learn about an organization's training and development needs, and may also develop manuals and presentations to assist employees in learning and practicing skills and counsel employees regarding their training needs.

Entry-level positions in this area include training specialist and orientation specialist. Training and development specialists conduct training sessions on communication, teamwork, and management, provide training, and maintain records of employee participation in training and development programs (Bureau of Labor Statistics, 2002). They help employees improve their knowledge and skills (e.g., sales techniques or safety guidelines) and assist supervisors and managers to improve their interpersonal skills in dealing with employees (Society for Human Resource Management, n.d.).

Employee Benefits and Services

The manager of personnel services, sometimes called HR director, or director of employee benefits and services, is responsible for administering employee benefits and services, including requests for vacation time, worker's compensation claims, and pension plans. In some organizations, personnel services direct recreational and social programs for employees. If you obtain a position in this area of human resources, you will spend time counseling employees on personal problems that relate to work, like whether and how to take a medical leave, open savings accounts for retirement, and apply for workers' compensation. You'll also need to keep abreast of changing regulations and legislation at the federal and state levels that have implications for employee benefits. Entry-level positions in this field are called employee assistance plan worker or specialist, and employee welfare specialist, though a variety of titles are used to describe these tasks.

Employee and Labor Relations

Many employees belong to a union, which allows them to bargain collectively with their employer and gain strength in numbers. Human resource workers in employee and labor relations work represent the organization and attempt to come to agreement with union representatives over all aspects of employee compensation, benefits, and contracts. They deal with collective bargaining, contract negotiations, and grievance settlement and arbitration. Typical titles are director of industrial relations, manager of labor relations, labor relations director, employee relations manager. Entry-level positions assist employee and labor relations management and are called employee and labor relations workers or specialists.

Human Resource Generalist

Though we've discussed the myriad areas in which human resource personnel work, smaller organizations often ask employees to engage in multiple human resource tasks, as generalists. Human resource generalists handle all aspects of personnel work and engage in a many activities including all of the preceding. They engage in recruitment, selection, placement, training, and development of employees. They may also administer salary and benefits, and develop personnel policies that conform to labor laws (Society for Human Resource Management, n.d.). Entry-level generalist positions typically fall under the following titles: human resource assistant, human resource specialist, personnel assistant, personnel specialist, or employee relations specialist. Of course, the director of human resources, the manager of all human resource functions in small and large organizations, is the ultimate human resources generalist.

EVALUATING HUMAN RESOURCE CAREERS

A career in human resources offers many advantages, including an office environment, 40-hour workweek, and opportunities for advancement. As a human resources employee, you'll have the opportunity to directly help people, solve practical problems, and use your knowledge of psychology. You will interact with a wide range of people in a position that requires flexibility, patience, and excellent communication skills (Society for Human Resource Management, n.d.). Sometimes the people part of the job can be stressful and challenging. For example, you'll have to deal with employees who are angry over changes in work conditions or who have been laid off. Some of your work as a human resources employee is crisis management—helping workers deal with sudden termination, sexual harassment, death of an employee, as well as more day-to-day stresses that can hamper job performance (Harcrow, 1998). Sometimes there will be little that you can do to help an employee, which can be frustrating. Of course, it feels very good when you are able to help an employee. Because human resources is about people, it is often unpredictable, demanding, and frustrating, but never boring.

Human resources positions entail administrative work and lots of paperwork that requires attention to detail and can sometimes be tedious. Some human resources positions, particularly those in recruitment and selection of employees, require extensive travel. Although human resources positions are highly competitive, the field is expected to grow as fast as the average for all occupations through 2010 (Bureau of Labor Statistics, 2002) and human resources positions are financially rewarding, as shown in Table 2.1.

TABLE 2.1   SALARIES IN HUMAN RESOURCES

Title	Median 2002 Salary
Entry-Level Positions	
Benefits analyst	$37,418
Employee relations specialist	$39,134
Employment representative	$36,782
HR generalist	$37,821
Human resources assistant	$26,263
Recruiter	$41,698
Training specialist	$38,344
Advanced Positions	
Employee relations specialist	$60,045
Employment representative	$53,848
HR generalist	$58,553
Organizational development specialist	$64,618
Recruiter	$68,453
Training specialist	$57,505
Managerial Positions	
Employment manager	$70,568
Employee relations manager	$73,876
HR manager	$71,399
Human resources director	$125,007
Organizational development manager	$83,509
Training manager	$70,519

(Adapted from Salary.com. 2003)

PREPARATION FOR HUMAN RESOURCE CAREERS

At the undergraduate level, psychology offers a solid background in communication skills, statistics, research methods, presentation skills, and human behavior that are needed for a career in human resources. Additional courses in industrial/organizational psychology, psychological measurement, communication, writing, business administration, labor law, and accounting will enhance your employability. Seek an internship to obtain experience and make contacts that can help you find an entry-level human resources position after graduation with your B.A. (Society for Human Resource Management, n.d.).

A master's degree in industrial or organizational psychology provides excellent preparation for more advanced positions in human resources. Courses in compensation, recruitment, training and development, performance appraisal, principles of management, and organizational structure are useful, as are courses in business administration. As with other entry-level positions, seek applied experiences during graduate school to make contacts with potential employers and develop and demonstrate your practical knowledge of the field. With a doctoral degree, or lots of experience, you'll be eligible for more advanced positions in human resources management.

Regardless of whether you're applying to entry-level or more advanced positions, there are a variety of personal qualities and skills that will help you to succeed in a human resources career. A good-natured, positive attitude, excellent speaking and writing skills, and the ability to work well with others are essential. As a human resources worker, you must be able to work with and supervise diverse people of various cultural, educational, and experiential backgrounds, and cope with conflicting views. Training in psychology at the undergraduate and graduate levels sensitizes graduates to the challenges of working with people and the importance of respecting all forms of diversity. Psychology graduates also understand how to gather information to determine what motivates employees and to devise plans to inspire excellent performance. If you're interested in industrial and organizational psychology, human resources careers offer opportunities to work within your area of interest at all levels of education.

Suggested Readings

Berry, L. M. (2003). *Employee selection.* Pacific Grove, CA: Wadsworth.

Katkowski, D. A., & Medsker, G. J. (2001). SIOP income and employment: Income and employment of SIOP members in 2000. *The Industrial/Organizational Psychologist.* Retrieved on November 8, 2003, from http://www.siop.org/tip/backissues/TipJul01/07salarysurvey.htm

McKenzie, J. S., Drinan, H. G., & Traynow, W. J. (2001). *Opportunities in human resource management careers.* New York: McGraw-Hill.

Pell, A. R. (1998). *The complete idiot's guide to managing people.* New York, NY: Alpha Books.

Tenopyr, M. L. (1997). Improving the workplace: Industrial/organizational psychology as a career. In R. Sternberg (Ed.), *Career paths in psychology: Where your degree can take you* (pp. 185–196). Washington, DC: American Psychological Association.

Traynor, W. J. & McKenzie, J. S. (1994). *Opportunities in human resource management careers.* Lincolnwood, IL: NTC Contemporary.

WEB RESOURCES

Academy of Management
   http://www.aomonline.org/

Society for Human Resource Management
   http://www.shrm.org/

Internet Survival Guide of Industrial/Organizational Psychology: Human Resource Management
   http://allserv.rug.ac.be/~flievens/hrm.htm

Job Analysis Internet Guide
   http://www.job-analysis.net/

Human Resources Career Profile
   http://www.wetfeet.com/asp/careerprofiles_overview.asp?careerpk=17

PROFILE: MARK KREMEN, M.S., INTERNAL CONSULTANT (SOURCE: AMMODT, 2004)

Organizations spend billions of dollars each year on training and development. As a consultant for a major financial institution, I play a part in the spending of those billions of dollars. However, I like to think of it as "investing" rather than spending. Like anything we invest in, we want to make sure we get a "pretty good" return on our investment. Training is no different. We do not want to be in a situation where the training dollars we spend are costing us more than the returns we receive. In this case, the returns are enhanced employee performance that can lead to increased company profits. As an internal consultant, I am responsible for ensuring that our organization gets a "pretty good" return from their training dollars. Just as many variables can affect your investments, many variables can also affect training.

   Training usually begins with a need. Whether it is introducing a new product or providing a more effective way to communicate, the training department is often called upon to support these issues. I work on developing partnerships with managers from other departments for the purpose of solving issues jointly, rather than having training being viewed as a "fix-all" department. I also provide managers with a checklist of questions they should be asking themselves before they call the training department to "fix" their problems. These questions will help the manager determine if training really is the answer to their problems.

   Creating these partnerships also helps with the transfer of learning back to the job. For example, before a team member attends a training program, it is necessary for that team member and his or her manager to have a discussion regarding the expectations and results of the training program he or she is about to attend. This enables the team member to become more focused on the knowledge and skills to be learned in the learning environment.

Once the team member enters the learning environment, I am responsible for facilitating the training program. Using such adult learning techniques as setting expectations, creating and maintaining interest, encouraging participation, and providing an opportunity for skill practice helps me create an environment that is conducive to learning. The majority of training programs I facilitate fall into the area of professional/management development as opposed to technical development. Some examples include supervision, communication, presentation, interviewing, and team-building skills.

I often work with a team of consultants with various backgrounds to develop new training programs. Depending on the type of program and the method of delivery, it can take many months to complete a new training program. Then, of course, we need to pilot the program and make adjustments accordingly. Sometimes an outside vendor may be used to assist us with a project. A training program is never really complete. There is always a fine-tuning that can be done to make the program more effective, especially if we are to customize a training program for a specific department.

Training does not end once the team member leaves the classroom. I follow up with team members and managers to determine if the knowledge and skills learned in the classroom are being applied back at the work area. I hold focus groups with managers and team members for the purpose of making the training program more effective. The manager also reinforces the learning by coaching and providing feedback to the team member. In some cases, especially for new hires, a mentor will be assigned to the team member for continuous on-the-job training. A mentor checklist will be provided to ensure standardization.

In addition to classroom training, I use other methods of enhancing performance. These include developing self-paced reading materials, creating job aids, and administering computer-based training. These methods are effective in that team members learn at their own pace and the materials can be assessed quickly as a reference for future needs.

To increase performance, it is important for me to understand our business goals and objectives and to align my consulting and training skills with them. At times, this may mean talking with a subject matter expert (SME) in an area I am working on for improved performance.

Measuring the improved performance is a necessary but often difficult task to accomplish. We use surveys, pre/postassessments, focus groups, and a wealth of reports from management to assist us with the measured results from our training program. Let's face it, some things are just plain easier to measure than others! However, this should not deter us from determining the impact our training program has on performance. The more accurately we can assess the impact our training programs has on improved performance, the more accurately we can link improved performance to profitability. After all, we want to make sure the training dollars we spend turn out to be a "pretty good" investment.

PROFILE: RHONDA DUFFLE, M.S., P.H.R., PFIZER (SOURCE: AMMODT, 2004)

I am the Manager of Operations for a distribution and fulfillment center in southwestern Virginia. We distribute samples and promotional materials for Pfizer, a large pharmaceutical and consumer health products manufacturer. In addition to my general operations duties, I am responsible for employee relations, employee training and development, compensation, benefits administration, employee recruitment, administration of selection tests, interviewing, employee orientation, and safety. Part of my time is spent recruiting and interviewing applicants for open positions. Recruiting and hiring highly qualified applicants is a critical component in the success of our operation, as well as the reputation of the human resources department.

Whether a position is a new or existing one, the first step is ensuring that an accurate job description exists for the position. Information from this job description is then used for recruitment. In advertising the position, it is important to target the appropriate market, which depends, in large part, on the type of position to be filled and the availability of qualified local applicants.

Because our center is located in a rural area, we sometimes have difficulty attracting qualified applicants for the upper-level positions. Therefore, it is essential to use a variety of recruitment methods to reach more potential applicants. All open positions are posted on the company's Web site, which includes a searchable database for all open positions. The job posting Web site allows internal and external candidates to search by location, facility, or job category. Candidates can complete an online application and may also attach a resume file to their online application. Pfizer also offers incentives to colleagues who refer candidates who are subsequently hired for positions with the company. In addition to the company Web site, a variety of other advertisement methods are used. For entry-level and mid-level positions, an advertisement is typically placed in a local newspaper. An employment ad is placed with the state employment office as well as with college placement offices. Recruiting for upper-level positions requires a broader focus. These positions are typically advertised regionally as well as nationally. Particularly for higher-level positions, we often utilize Web-based job posting sites such as Monster.com.

As with most organizations, an important part of the selection process is the employment interview. To increase the effectiveness of the interview as a selection tool, we use a structured interview for all open positions. For each position, a set of essential competencies is identified. Questions for each competency are established and may be either technical or situational in nature. Applicants are interviewed by a member of the HR staff, then by the position's supervisor, and lastly, by another supervisor. Each interviewer takes notes during the interview and completes a standard rating sheet with ratings for each of the identified competencies. Using a structured interview and having several independent interviewers increases the amount of pertinent information received and reduces the bias involved in typical interviews. Depending upon the position, applicants also may be required to pass typing, data-entry, or PC skills assessments. Once an offer of employment is made, the candidate is required to complete a physical and substance abuse screening test. In addition, criminal background checks are conducted for all new hires. This is to ensure that there are no criminal record issues, that may prelude a colleague from working in certain positions, such as handling prescription drugs.

CONSULTANT

CHAPTER GUIDE

Consultant is an umbrella term for a variety of professionals who help others solve sophisticated problems in business, research, industry, and government settings. Most consultants develop niche specialties. For example, organizational consultants specialize in how to improve organizational functioning and executive search consultants focus on evaluating and hiring individuals for leadership positions within organizations. Research consultants use their methodological and statistical skills to help organizations, businesses, and government gather information and analyze it. Some industrial and organizational psychologists consult as expert witnesses; they provide expert witness testimony in court. In this chapter we'll examine the world of consulting for industrial and organizational psychologists.

MANAGEMENT CONSULTANT

Management consulting is a broad term for many consulting careers. Management consultants apply a scientific approach of hypothesis testing and data analysis to solve business problems. They provide businesses and corporations with advice and assistance in researching new markets, reorganizing a company's structure, hiring top executives, and other management issues. Because management must deal with many concerns, management consulting offers diverse opportunities. Consultants often specialize in specific management concerns, such as strategy, operations, information technology, and human resources. For example, consider the following types of management consultants:

- Strategic management consultants advise companies on business strategy, such as how to grow a business, what operations to perform, whether to enter new geographic markets, launch new products, buy other businesses, and so on.

- Operations management consultants study how to improve operational efficiency, including how to reduce waste and improve productivity.

- Information technology consultants advise organizations about technology issues, such as whether their accounting software meets their needs, how to manage the vast amounts of information needed for operations, and how to create and organize databases for maximum efficiency and security.

- Executive search consultants are high-level recruiters, often called "headhunters," who use their knowledge of industrial and organizational psychology to recruit, assess, and place employees in top positions.

- Organizational development consultants help companies with team building, training (e.g., teaching communication and conflict management skills), dealing with change, and professional development.

All management consultants work with clients to help them develop and implement strategies for success—whether in organizational development, marketing, information technology, or other areas. Management consultants offer their clients problem analysis, perspective and insight, recommendations, and strategic plans for achieving change. They often work with other consultants or company employees to analyze a problem and brainstorm potential solutions. They then develop initial hypotheses and test them through logical analysis and research. Management consultants collect information from articles, surveys, and interviews, and analyze the collected data to draw conclusions. Then, they communicate their findings and recommendations, and work with clients to implement solutions.

Advantages and Disadvantages of Management Consulting

A primary advantage of a career in management consulting is that you'll always be encouraged to learn new things. Every project brings new challenges and opportunities. Many management consultants explain that there is a steep learning curve in that each project may require you to learn about a new field and certainly a new company. You'll meet and work with many people of diverse backgrounds, training, and interests. The people part of management consulting, communicating with others and solving interpersonal problems, can be stimulating, but also exhausting—especially because there's no predicting how a company's employees will react to your presence. Some will embrace you and your efforts to help them improve; others may be wary and may be unhelpful. Even entry-level management consultants are given much responsibility as well as exposure to a company's senior executives. Your suggestions are heard and can make a big difference. Alternatively, the responsibility can be overwhelming as you'll be held accountable for errors and misjudgments.

Management consulting usually entails a great deal of travel. You'll travel to where your clients are located, sometimes spending weeks conducting research or implementing solutions on the road. Business travel can be glamorous, but it can also strain relationships with family and friends. Management consulting is hard work requiring creativity and dedication. Long hours (55–70 per week) are common and the overall pace of work is fast. The travel, long hours, and stress of a career in management consulting are matched by high salaries. The mean income for all consultants is $74,600 (career journal.com, n.d.). Among doctoral-level industrial/organizational psychologist consultants, the median salary in 2001 was $92,500 (Singleton, Tate, & Randall, 2003). Though consulting is a competitive field, it's expected to grow faster than the average for all occupations through 2010 (Bureau of Labor Statistics, 2002).

Preparing for a Career in Management Consulting

As a psychology graduate, you are well suited to careers in consulting because you have advanced analytical skills. You understand how to analyze data, manage databases, and present data simply and elegantly through the use of tables and graphs. Your knowledge of computer software and statistics is an asset to any organization, and your communication skills, honed through writing papers, theses, and dissertations, as well as making conference presentations, are valuable in the office setting (Sebestyen, 2000). Your understanding of psychological theories and "how people work" are assets, but you need to be able to apply your understanding and explain it to businesspeople in ways that they can understand and appreciate. Because teamwork is an essential part of the job of management consultant, your interpersonal skills, and understanding of group dynamics and leadership will come in handy.

Employers, however, may not be familiar with psychology at the bachelor's or graduate level, so you must "sell" your degree. Communicate your strengths to potential employers. Also, make contacts, get experience, and meet potential employers by completing an internship with a management consulting firm. Finally, be introspective and evaluate whether management consulting is for you. The people who are happiest in consulting careers are intellectually curious and enjoy problem solving, like constant change, like dealing with ambiguous environments where they need to find structure for themselves, and don't mind extensive travel (Weetfeet.com, 2003).

RESEARCH CONSULTANT

By now you're well aware of the research skills that industrial, organizational, and human factors psychologists bring to the table. Many work as research consultants, providing advice on methodology and statistics to businesses, industry, and government. In Chapter 2 we discussed psychologists as researchers, so here we focus on using research in business settings.

Market Research

Market researchers are found in a variety of organizations including public relations firms, advertising agencies, and corporations. They conduct research on the sale of a product or service and analyze data on past sales to predict future sales and trends. Market researchers design methods of gathering information on products or services, as well as consumers' needs, tastes, purchasing power, and buying habits. They examine consumer reactions to products and services. Through interview, focus group, and survey research, they identify advertising needs, measure the effectiveness of advertising and other promotional techniques, gather data on competitors' products, services, and locations, and analyze their marketing methods and strategies (Careers in Business, 2000). Market researchers who work for public relations firms and in government positions often conduct opinion research to determine public attitudes on various issues, which may help political and business leaders evaluate public support for their positions or advertising policies (Bureau of Labor Statistics, 2002).

Careers in market research are fast-paced and exciting. Market researchers work on a variety of different projects and project turnover is fast. The research often is needed quickly as clients must make business decisions (Yund, 1998). Some of the work can be tedious and you'll need to be able to attend to details because much of your time will be spent on data analysis. Patience, persistence, and the ability to work alone is needed as you'll spend many hours in independent study and problem solving. An important benefit to a career in market research is that your work holds practical implications. Companies will make decisions about products, advertising strategies, and marketing based on your work. Overall, market research is a growth field. Employment of market researchers is expected to grow faster than the average for all occupations through 2010 (Bureau of Labor Statistics, 2002). Finally, salaries in market research are very competitive. In 2003, a typical market research analyst earned a median base salary of $49,379; half of the people in this job earn between $44,088 and $58,110 (Salary.com, 2003).

With a bachelor's degree, you're eligible for entry-level positions in marketing as a research assistant. A graduate degree will prepare you for higher-level positions in market research. Additional courses in business, marketing, consumer behavior, mathematics, statistics, sampling theory, survey design, and computer science are extremely helpful. Interpersonal communications classes are useful because you'll need to be able to work well with others as you may conduct or oversee interviews for a wide variety of individuals. You also must be able to present your findings, both orally and in writing, in a clear, concise manner, so your training in psychology coupled with classes in writing and English offer important preparation.

Data Mining

Data mining refers to the extraction of useful information, or "nuggets," from large databases of information with the use of statistical methods and computational algorithms. It's essentially finding a needle in a haystack, wherein the needle is critical information that an organization needs and the haystack is the large database with information stored over a long period of time. Data mining entails using statistical analysis to examine large databases for patterns and trends that shed light on consumer habits and potential marketing strategies.

Data mining is used in all industries. For example, discovering new patterns and trends through data mining can help banking executives to "predict with increasing precision how customers will react to interest rate adjustments, which customers will be most receptive to new product offers, which customers present the highest risk for defaulting on a loan, and how to make each customer relationship more profitable" (Fabris, 1998).

Data mining professionals, sometimes called data warehousing professionals or database analysts, are in high demand in order to develop highly targeted marketing programs, analyze economic trends, detect credit fraud, and forecast financial markets. It's a challenging career that requires analytic thinking and problem-solving skills. The main challenges of a career in data mining and data warehousing are the stresses of meeting goals, rolling out database upgrades, learning new analysis techniques, long hours, and analyzing data and drawing conclusions on tight deadlines and with limited budgets and staffs (Smith, 2002). According to Information Week (2002) a typical person working in the data mining and warehousing field earned a median base salary of $70,500 in 2002. Salary.com (2003) estimates the median salary of a database analyst as $72,983 in 2003.

Psychology graduates with strong interests in data management should consider careers in data mining. Graduate degrees aren't necessary, but they are helpful as they indicate advanced reasoning and statistical expertise. If you're interested in a career in data mining, learn about the most popular databases, like SQL, DB2, and Oracle—the key to a career in data mining is learning the popular databases, so develop your expertise (Joss, 2000). Research technical education programs because there are many programs that allow you to take weeklong courses that introduce you to database administration on your choice of platforms. These courses are expensive but offer a quick avenue to expand your knowledge, get certified in a particular database, and enhance your credentials.

EXECUTIVE COACH

An executive coach is a consultant who focuses on developing executive's leadership skills (Kilburg, 1996). Executive coaching is similar to management consulting; however, the emphasis is on the individual executive as opposed to the organization at large (Garman, Whiston, & Zlatoper, 2000). Executive coaches work one-on-one with executives and focus on making leaders more effective by helping them to identify and address their strengths and weaknesses, and enhance leadership and management skills (Witherspoon & White, 1996). An executive coach might assist a manager who has never supervised before, serve as a sounding board for strategic decision making, or help a manager cope with stress (Foxhall, 2002).

If you're interested in becoming an executive coach, recognize that there is no universally accepted certification for executive coaching; nor are there standard definitions of coaching or regulations governing good practice (Garman et al., 2000). A master's degree in industrial or organizational psychology (or even clinical or counseling psychology) coupled with experience in the business world and an understanding of leadership and management in organizational settings will prepare you for a career as an executive coach. A doctoral degree substantially aids your credentials. Becoming an executive coach requires eclectic training. If you've been trained in industrial or organizational psychology, you must learn more about clinical and developmental issues that can influence a leader's effectiveness (and vice versa if you're coming from a clinical or counseling background). You must have an interest in business and understand the demands of leadership roles (Foxhall, 2003), so seek internships in business settings and apprenticeship relationships with experienced executive coaches (Glasser, 2002). Executive coaches help managers and leaders develop interpersonal skills, so excellent interpersonal and relational skills are essential. Also seek to develop skills in active listening, objective setting, creating action plans, and evaluating implementation plans and interventions (Glasser, 2002).

A career as an executive coach offers constant change, challenges, and independence. Coaching is conducted in person and by phone, so there's a tremendous amount of flexibility. Most executive coaches have independent practices, but some are employed as internal coaches for organizations or for consulting firms. If you seek an independent practice, expect to spend significant resources and time on marketing and developing a client base. Once established, a career as an executive coach is lucrative. Most executive coaches charge between $200 and $500 per hour (Grodzki, 2002). Because coaching is an umbrella term similar to management consulting, it's important for psychologists who coach to remain vigilant in assessing their own competence and communicate with clients regarding exactly what types of problems they are qualified to work on (Foxhall, 2003). Finally, executive coaching receives lots of media attention and is a growing career field (Garman, et al., 2000).

EXPERT WITNESS

Expert witnesses testify as part of an attorney's presentation of the evidence in a court setting. Expert witnesses "possess special knowledge about a topic, knowledge that the average juror does not have" (Wrightsman, 2001, p. 32). The expert's role is "to educate the judge or jury as to the relevance of the psychological knowledge on the topic in general and the specific psychological findings relevant to the questions being asked in the particular case" (Walker, 1990, p. 351).

Industrial, organizational, and human factors psychologists are called on to provide testimony on a variety of topics, such as negligence and product liability (e.g., Does the environment or our perceptual abilities influence how we use the product or what precautions we take in using the product?), trademark litigation (e.g., Is the product's name or packaging so similar to a competitor's that it may be confusing for consumers? Are advertising claims misleading?), and stereotyping, statistics, validation, and performance and appraisal systems (Harris, 2000; Neitzel & Dillehay, 1986). The expert's job is to present a balanced and neutral view of the relevant literature and draw conclusions based on scientifically validated methodologies and theoretical positions (Rotgers & Barrett, 1996). The expert witness acts as educator in that he or she provides testimony that explains complicated psychological issues to help the jurors to understand the issues and uncover the truth.

If you're considering pursuing a career as an expert witness, recognize that generally a doctoral degree is the standard credential and most psychologists who provide expert testimony do so as one of many roles. For example, researchers and college professors provide expert testimony regarding areas of their research, as do high-level human resources personnel. It's unlikely that you will devote your entire career to providing expert testimony. Instead, your role as an expert witness will be one of the many roles that you'll fulfill as a psychologist (e.g., educator, researcher, consultant).With that said, expert testimony provides many advantages. One of the most salient advantages is that it is lucrative. Expert witnesses may earn as much as $500 per hour, depending on specialty area and experience (Wrightsman et al., 2002).

A potential drawback is that taking the witness stand is challenging, to say the least. The cross-examination will likely challenge your experience, credentials, person, and the validity of your professional work. Lloyd-Bostock (1988) explains that, "the treatment psychologists… are sometimes exposed to in the witness box can come as a shock to the unprepared" (p. 432). Providing testimony can be both intimidating and exciting, and requires professionalism and emotional control. Many psychologists thrive within an adversarial courtroom environment, whereas others dread it.

Another potential disadvantage to providing expert testimony is that you must have "eyes in the back of your head." Cross-examining attorneys may attempt to discredit you in the eyes of the jury by reading excerpts of your articles aloud, citing information from your interviews or television appearances, and any other information that they can find to demonstrate inconsistency in your work, opinions, and conclusions. Essentially this means that if you decide to provide expert testimony, you must carefully examine your career for any information (professional or personal) that might be used to discredit you in the eyes of the jury (Reid, 1999). Therefore, a potential disadvantage to becoming an expert witness is a loss of privacy in one's professional and personal life. Nevertheless, serving as an expert witness is intellectually stimulating and, for some, invigorating.

A final challenge to a career as an expert witness is coping with the fact that the nature of law and psychology often collide. The law expects firm either/or decisions, while psychology discusses probabilities and likelihoods rather than black-and-white decisions. In other words, "the law requires the psychologist to reach a firm conclusion on the witness stand, regardless of ambiguity in the evidence" (Wrightsman et al., 2002, p. 44). As a student of psychology, you've come to understand that behavior is influenced by multiple factors and that there is rarely one cause to a particular behavior or event. Psychologists who take the witness stand must traverse the ambiguity to arrive at conclusions, and then explain how they arrived at the conclusions as well as the limiting factors. This is a difficult task indeed.

SUGGESTED READINGS

Fitzgerald, C., & Berger, J. G. (2002). *Executive coaching: Practices and perspectives.* Palo Alto, CA: Consulting Psychologists Press.

Garfein, R. (1997) An interesting career in psychology: International marketing research consultant. *Psychological Science Agenda.* Retrieved May 23, 2003 from http://www.apa.org/science/ic-garfein.html

Glaser, D. (2001). An interesting career in psychology: Statistical and methodological consultant. *Psychological Science Agenda.* Retrieved May 23, 2003 from http://www.apa.org/science/ic-glaser.html

Heckler, V. J. (1998). On being helped to become a management psychologist: Partially paying back a debt of gratitude. *Consulting Psychology Journal: Practice and Research, 50,* 255–262.

Kilburg, R. R. (1996). Toward a conceptual understanding and definition of executive coaching. *Consulting Psychology Journal: Practice and Research, 48,* 134–144.

Kraus, S. J. (1996). An interesting career in psychology: Market research consultant. *Psychological Science Agenda.* Retrieved May 23, 2003 from http://www.apa.org/science/ic-kraus.html

Mannila, H., Smyth, P., & Hand, D. J. (2001). *Principles of data mining.* Cambridge, MA: MIT Press.

Metzger, R. O. (1993). *Developing a consulting practice.* Thousand Oaks, CA: Sage.

Naifcy, M. (1997). *The fast track: The insider's guide to winning jobs in management consulting, investment banking, and securities trading.* New York, NY: Broadway Books.

Poynter, D. (1997). *Expert witness handbook: Tips and techniques for the litigation consultant.* Santa Barbara, CA: Para Publishing.

Schwartz, N. (1995). An interesting career in psychology: Executive search consultant. *Psychological Science Agenda.* Retrieved May 23, 2003 from http://www.apa.org/science/ic-schwartz.html

Smith, P. M. (1997). An interesting career in psychology: Organizational development consultant. *Psychological Science Agenda.* Retrieved May 23, 2003 from http://www.apa.org/science/ic-smith.html

Stapp, J. (1996). An interesting career in psychology: Trial Consultant. *Psychological Science Agenda.* Retrieved August 15, 2002 from http://www.apa.org/science/ic-stapp.html

WEB RESOURCES

Careers in Consulting
    http://www.careers-in-business.com/consulting/mc.htm

Management Consulting
    http://www.columbia.edu/cu/ccs/99website/99student/exploration/research/capsules/consulting/

Data Mining: What Is Data Mining?
    http://www.anderson.ucla.edu/faculty/jason.frand/teacher/technologies/palace/datamining.htm

The Data Warehousing Information Center
    http://www.dwinfocenter.org/

Expert Testimony Articles
    http://www.denison.edu/psych/psychlaw/testimony/

Institute of Management Consultants
    http://www.imcusa.org

PROFILE: AMY PODURGAL, M.S., SQUARE PEG CONSULTING, INC. (SOURCE: AMMODT, 2004)

I am the owner and president of Square Peg Consulting, Inc., an organization and training development consulting company. After earning my master's degree in I/O psychology, I spent 7 years working in the pharmaceutical industry as both a training and development specialist and an organization development consultant. At Glaxo, I designed and delivered management development training programs as well as provided organization development consultation to senior management teams. I also helped launch Glaxo's Total Quality Management (TQM) and process improvement programs in their Technical Operations division. While employed at Merck and Co., Inc., I designed and delivered training and employee involvement programs including facilitating employee involvement teams.

After leaving the pharmaceutical industry, I worked at Nortel Networks. I began as a senior manager in Human Resources and Organization Development, leading the effort in starting up two new businesses for Nortel, one of which is now a significant part of Nortel's strategic data business portfolio. This included benchmarking Silicon Valley technology companies and developing and aligning HR and organization systems to business goals to create a new entrepreneurial culture that positioned Nortel as a competitive business and employer.

I then served as a Senior Manager in several areas including Customer Value Management, Sales and Marketing, and Human Resources and Organization Development. My last position involved working directly with Nortel customers and Nortel Account Management teams to align Nortel's organization processes with identified customer value drives to achieve full customer potential.

I left Nortel to start my own consulting firm, Square Peg Consulting, Inc., where I work with clients to improve the effectiveness of their organizations. I use a whole-systems approach to organizational development (OD), focusing on organization alignment as the key to organization effectiveness. A systems approach includes viewing the organization as a living organism, influenced by external and internal elements. There is a cause-and-effect relationship between each element, and organizations are most effective when all the systems within it align. My approach to enabling organizations to better perform is to assess alignment gaps and opportunities and develop interventions that align resources, systems, and processes to better position the organization to achieve business results. Because organizations grow and evolve through their natural organizational life cycle, it is important that they continue to shift and realign themselves to ensure all their efforts are going in the same direction for maximum efficiency and effectiveness.

One important element of organizational effectiveness is communication. From a diagnostic perspective, one can tell much about an organization's culture from assessing both what and how communication is shared throughout the organization. For example, if an organization claims to have a culture of "empowerment," yet employees are not aware of the organization's goals or vision, there is a potential gap between leadership's intention and the reality in which employees live. As a result, dysfunctional behavior may occur, leading to mistrust and poor performance.

Confusion and dissatisfaction arise when an organization's communication and governance practices are incongruent with the culture they espouse. For instance, a company aspiring to engage employees in the business while restricting employee access to information about its financial performance may be viewed cynically by employees. A company proclaiming to trust and empower employees while limiting delegation of authority may be perceived as disingenuous.

Think of the organization's communications strategy as a three-legged stool. One leg is its external communications strategy—the messages sent to the outside world about the organization's product or service offerings, including competitive differentiators, market space and positioning, and financial performance. This type of communication helps brand the company in the eyes of current and future customers, shareholders, and job candidates. It includes such things as the company's external Web site, its marketing materials, and its media relation's activities.

The second leg represents the internal communications strategy. This communication strategy ensures that employees stay informed about the performance of the company, important changes to policies and practices, and can serve as a vehicle for recognizing employee and team accomplishments. The company newsletter, its intranet site, and its approach to organizing employee meetings are all components of an internal communications strategy.

The third leg is the organization alignment strategy, the organized method by which the organization's strategy and tactics are developed and communicated to employees. This helps drive the daily activities of employees and ensures that they are all working in support of the organization's priorities. This usually takes the form of objective setting and performance management and is where the strategic and operational elements of an organization meet. For organizations to be effective, all three legs of the communications stool must be strategically aligned and working together.

Organizations are living organisms whose systems and structures are set up to accomplish a goal. A publicly traded company's goal may be to grow shareholder value, a sports team's goal may be to win the game, and a symphony's goal may be to master a piece of music. An effective communication strategy, one that takes into account the information needs of all constituents in each part of the system, is a critical and often overlooked element for ensuring alignment and, ultimately, organizational success.

PROFILE: HEATHER KING FOSTER, M. A., TOWERS PERRIN (SOURCE: AMMODT, 2004)

Towers Perrin is an international human resources and management consulting firm whose vision is to be the supplier of choice for financial and actuarial services, benefits and retirement services, people strategy and research, communication, change, and total rewards. Our firm has 135 years of experience in several of these service areas, allowing us to bring value-added consulting expertise to our clients. As a firm, our mission is to build relationships with and improve business performance results for our clients.

I am a consultant in our Organizational and Employee Research line of business. In this line of business we conduct research through surveys, focus groups, and interviews. These data are used in a variety of ways to solicit input, understand perceptions, improve performance, and gain buy-in. Our research is generally used to help organizations align their spending on employee programs with what employees value, decrease turnover, increase employment engagement or satisfaction, and improve communication or productivity.

Although we can conduct a variety of research on any given project, we work with our clients to determine which method, or combination of methods, would best meet their budget, timing, and overall project needs. On some projects we suggest that the client simply conduct an employee survey or focus groups. With others, we recommend they also interview key executives and possibly use ongoing feedback to collect data periodically as changes are implemented.

An organization that decides to undergo the full range of employee research may decide to develop an integrated plan for involving key stakeholders over a period of time. This integrated approach typically starts by engaging the top executives through an interview process. Our research team will partner with the client team and our own colleagues in other lines of business, such as change, communication, benefits, and compensation, to develop a guide to be used during the interviews. The questions in this guide explore executives'

- perceptions of the business and the role employees play in business success.

- philosophy of the rewards programs—what they should be designed to do or not do; for example, should rewards programs be a factor in an employee's decision to join the organization? Stay with an organization? Become fully engaged in his or her work?

- assessment of the impact major changes have had on the organization and its employees.

- views of where the organization's programs should rank against other organizations.

- guidance for the current project team and measures of success.

The data gathered from executives are typically used to set the direction for the project, and input gathered from other groups along the way is compared to these data.

Another core group often targeted for research efforts is line managers. These leaders are typically closest to employees and have the greatest influence on the communication employees receive. By involving managers early in the process, typically through focus groups, we gain an understanding of their needs and challenges as managers; the role that rewards programs play in their ability to attract, retain, and engage employees; and how their views align with those of executives.

Employees often participate in a major change effort through a survey. Input from the executive interviews and manager focus groups are combined with data gathered through employee focus groups to develop the survey. The survey is then administered either to the entire employee population or to a sample of employees. The more sensitive and pervasive the change effort, the more likely the client will want to provide every employee with a chance to participate. We conduct surveys using a variety of methods: Web, paper, email, and telephone. Once the survey is administered and data are received, we conduct a number of statistical analyses to understand the data. We look at differences across demographic groups, create indices of items to understand "drivers" of employee perceptions, and look for general trends in the data. Our analyses are then used to write a detailed report of the results, where we pull together all the data that has been gathered thus far on the project. We explain the point of view from executives, to managers, to employees, and we compare and contrast their perceptions on various issues.

Often we follow an employee survey with focus groups. These focus groups are used to further explore issues identified in the survey and can be used to test ideas for change or communication with employees. Another form of gathering additional data from employees is through pulse surveys. These surveys are often administered online to just a sample of employees and are brief in nature. Pulse surveys allow the client to gather quick, "real time" data to gauge employees' perceptions and understanding of changes and communication messages that have been introduced. These results are tracked over time to monitor progress that has been made within the organization as a result of a major change.

The most critical component of any form of research is the client's willingness to use the data. Organizations that are the best examples for using employee research ask their employees for feedback on a regular basis, have a good track record for using the data, and constantly keep employees informed of its use.

PROFILE: HILARY R. WEINER, PH.D., EQUAL EMPLOYMENT OPPORTUNITY COMMISSION (SOURCE: PSYCHOLOGICAL SCIENCE AGENDA, 2001)

While my career has had many interesting twists and turns, I consider my present job as an expert witness with the Equal Employment Opportunity Commission (EEOC) to be my most rewarding. It offers me an opportunity to use virtually all of the skills I have developed during my education and later experience in helping investigators and attorneys determine whether or not employment discrimination has taken place. I also get to persuade others of my opinions, which are based on analyses specifically related to the cases, as well as the published research in my field.

Currently, I work as an in-house testifying expert for EEOC. My involvement in a case usually begins with a telephone call from an attorney in one of our district offices, which are located in major cities across the United States. In most instances, the office has received multiple complaints about a particular employer, and the attorney wants to know whether there is statistical support for filing a class action discrimination lawsuit in court. In other instances, a test or other employment selection procedure has been found to have adverse impact against a group protected by Title VII of the Civil Rights Act, and the attorney wants me to review validation studies for adherence to current professional standards, as required by the Uniform Guidelines on Employee Selection Procedures. In either case, I provide guidance to the office in obtaining and analyzing the information they need to determine whether discrimination has taken place. If a lawsuit is filed against an employer, I am often called to testify at the deposition and trial concerning the results of my analyses and related expert opinions.

When a lawsuit is filed in a class action discrimination case, it usually goes through a fairly long "discovery" phase before going to trial. The purpose of discovery is for both sides to find out as much as they can about the actions of the other side and to develop evidence that they will use at trial. During the discovery phase, I typically help EEOC trial attorneys obtain computerized data needed to perform statistical analyses and company documents which may contain information about hiring, promotion, salary, demotion, and/or layoff decisions (depending on the basis of the case). I also provide questions to be used during depositions of key company officials and sometimes attend those depositions.

On the basis of the information obtained during discovery, I perform appropriate statistical analyses and write a report concerning those analyses and my resulting opinions. More often than not, the defendant company also has one or more experts who perform the same tasks for the other side and who are deposed by EEOC or other plaintiffs' attorneys.

The defendant's attorneys have the opportunity to depose or question me under oath concerning the content of my report and my qualifications to provide expert opinions on the matters contained in my report. Since the goal of the opposing attorney is to discredit the expert, depositions are probably the most difficult aspect of my job. Some of the more aggressive attorneys will attempt to rattle an expert by making accusations concerning lack of professionalism and incompetence. However, as long as the expert understands the game-playing aspect of the deposition, doesn't take the accusations personally, and sticks to the analysis and report, it is an unpleasant situation that can be survived.

Most of the cases I have been involved in have settled before trial. Often, the monetary amount of settlement and other remedial actions are based on information provided by the experts for the plaintiff and defendant in their reports and at deposition. When a case does go to trial, it is either heard in front of a judge or a jury. The expert is questioned by his or her own attorney (direct examination), then cross-examined by the opposing attorney. Direct examination is very predictable because you can only testify concerning matters in your expert reports, and you have likely worked with the attorney in formulating the kinds of questions to ask. Cross-examination is similar to deposition, but, by this time, you have already been through the war and can anticipate what will be asked.

Obviously, serving as an expert witness in class action employment discrimination cases is not an entry-level job for a Ph.D. psychologist. It is necessary to have several years of experience performing applied research and/or working as an industrial/organizational (I/O) psychologist with experience in personnel selection. Before coming to EEOC, I worked as a survey statistician and as a personnel psychologist for the federal government. Other psychologists have become testifying experts after working as I/O psychologists in the private sector or in academia.

A career as a testifying expert in employment discrimination cases is a path that I would recommend to psychologists with strong analytical skills and a desire for challenging work. The amount of variety in the work is almost unparalleled. In addition to everything else, I have the knowledge that what I do is serving a valuable societal purpose, a great bonus in any career choice.

Source: Weiner, H. R. (October, 2001). An Interesting Career in Psychology: Expert Witness in Employment Discrimination Cases. Psychological Science Agenda (available at http://www.apa.org/science/ic-weiner.html)

PRODUCT DEVELOPMENT AND ENVIRONMENTAL DESIGN

CHAPTER GUIDE

Many students with interests in human factors psychology seek careers in product development and environmental design. Human factors is the study of the interaction between humans and things—how people interact with their environments, objects, and machines. Human factors psychologists are often employed by companies to improve the user friendliness of designs (Aamodt, 2004). They might choose the best layout for a computer keyboard, design book bags to distribute weight evenly on the wearer, or design work gloves that maximize safety to workers without reducing performance. In the workplace, human factors psychologists design environments in order to optimize productivity, employee satisfaction, and safety, and limit stress, fatigue, and error. In this chapter we explore careers related to human factors.

COMMERCIAL OR INDUSTRIAL DESIGN ASSISTANT

With a bachelor's degree in psychology, you might seek a position as an assistant to a commercial or industrial designer. In this position, you would help in designing products and equipment, such as cars, children's toys, computer equipment, furniture, home appliances, and medical, office, and recreational equipment. A designer combines artistic talent with research on customer needs, how products are used, the consumer market, and production materials and methods to a design that is functional, appealing, and competitive with others in the marketplace. An assistant to a designer conducts research related to the designer's needs. Design assistants help the designer to coordinate design concepts among engineering, marketing, production, and sales departments in order to produce a product that is safe, well-designed, and marketable. Depending on the particular field or industry, design assistants may help designers in planning packaging and containers for products, such as foods, beverages, toiletries, or medicine, or might assist in creating and designing packaging, illustrations, or advertising for manufactured materials.

Designers and design assistants are employed by manufacturers, corporations, and design firms. They tend to work regular 40-hour weeks in an office setting. Because design is an area of growth, the market for design assistants will grow through the year 2010 (Bureau of Labor Statistics, 2002). In 2002, the median entry level salary in design was $30,400 (American Institute of Graphic Arts, 2002).

If you're interested in becoming a design assistant, creativity is essential and sketching ability will help you to advance to design positions. Psychology's emphasis on research methods and problem solving will suit you well in this field. In addition, take courses in merchandising, business administration, marketing, and seek training in art—especially a course in computer-aided design.

Although a bachelor's degree in psychology prepares graduates for entry-level jobs, graduate-degree holders have more opportunities for advancement.

A master's degree offers a wide range of opportunities in human factors, usability, and market research careers. Doctoral degrees offer additional opportunities, especially in upper management, consulting, and product design and development careers; however, individuals with master's degrees and extensive experience often obtain positions comparable to doctoral-degree holders.

USABILITY SPECIALIST

Many psychologists with graduate degrees in industrial/organizational or human factors psychology obtain positions in product design and development. These psychologists specialize in promoting product usability, or the ease and pleasantness of use. Usable, or user-friendly, products are easy for users to learn how to use, are efficient and memorable, minimize errors, and are pleasing or satisfying to use (Aamodt, 2004). Usability specialists ensure that product designs fit users. They work with all kinds of products: toys, computer hardware and software, electronic equipment, cars, and more.

Psychologists who work in product design and production use their understanding of human capabilities and limitations to advocate for users so that products are designed to meet the needs of the user (Day, 1996). They research a product, create product prototypes, test them, and modify them based on input from potential users. For example, in designing the interior of an automobile, a psychologist might create a life-size prototype in which all of the instruments and controls can be moved (e.g., by attaching them with Velcro). Potential users then provide feedback on the best location for each of the instruments and controls, moving them as necessary. Other psychologists conduct these types of usability studies to create aircraft that meet pilots' needs and thereby reduce pilot error (Lauber, 1997; Tyler, 2000). Usability studies are also employed in designing all kinds of products, like computer software and hardware, kitchen utensils, appliances, writing products (e.g., ergonomic pens), "childproof" caps for medication, and many more products that we use every day.

Psychologists who choose careers in product design and development have the opportunity to engage in research that improves people's experiences with products. Their research has practical implications and they get to see the results of their work. A regular 40-hour workweek schedule, overall growth of the profession (Bureau of Labor Statistics, 2002), excellent opportunities for master's-level psychologists, and high rates of compensation are other advantages. In 2000, the average salary for usability practitioners was $70,094 (Usability Professionals Association, 2001). In 2001, the estimated starting salary for usability professionals was $67,118, with an additional $2,265 for each year of experience (Nielsen Norman Group, 2001).

ENVIRONMENTAL DESIGNER

Environmental design entails studying the interactive relationship between environments and human behavior. Why do people find some spaces comfortable and others threatening? Why are some spaces easier to navigate than others? Environmental designers study these questions and apply what they learn to design and enhance environments, such as the lay-out of offices, the design of office buildings and shopping malls, and even the design of neighborhoods and communities, to reduce stress, create more efficiency, and minimize accidents.

Psychologists with interests in environmental design work for corporations, local and federal governments, and consulting firms. Some participate in city and community planning, designing buildings, and enhancing the interior layout of existing structures. A career in environmental design requires good communication skills and the ability to work as part of a team. Environmental designers who are assigned to large projects will work closely with professionals from many different fields, such as politicians, architects, urban planners, economists, and engineers, to complete projects. Working with many disciplines can be very interesting, but also challenging. Good listening skills and research skills are essential to success in this field because environmental designers spend lots of time interacting with people—consumers and community members in addition to other professionals. For example, when a city plans to rebuild a rundown neighborhood, psychologists may interview people who live in the neighborhood to hear their ideas and perspectives about how to improve the area.

As you might imagine, an important advantage of a career in environmental design is the opportunity to be part of a large project and make a difference. An environmental designer who participates in designing a new community housing project, for example, will find that their work influences residents' day-to-day lives. But the teamwork needed to complete large-scale projects can sometimes lead to frustration because when many people are involved, decisions can take a very long time. Also, projects generally take a long time to implement, which can be challenging for someone who is looking for more immediate results from their work. Environmental designers who can take criticism well and to deal with pressure without becoming overly stressed are at a distinct advantage in this often stressful field.

Careers in environmental design are expected to increase about as fast as average through the year 2010 (Bureau of Labor Statistics, 2002), and salaries are competitive. In 1999, the average salary for a doctoral-level psychologist in environmental design was over $65,000 ($71,000 adjusted for 2002; Conaway, 2000). If you're interested in a career in environmental design, a master's degree in human factors psychology will provide you with the research skills to enter this field. Seek additional training in communications, research design and statistics, and related fields, such as economics, urban planning, and architecture. Also seek an internship with an environmental design firm, city planning office, or related placement to obtain hands-on experience in this exciting field.

SUGGESTED READINGS

Beall, A. E., & Allen, T. W. (1997). Why we buy what we buy: Consulting in consumer psychology. In R. Sternberg (Ed.), *Career paths in psychology: Where your degree can take you* (pp. 197–212). Washington, DC: American Psychological Association.

Hannah, B. (2003). *Becoming a product designer: A guide to careers in design.* Hoboken, NJ: Wiley.

Mencher, M. (2002). *Get in the game: Careers in the game industry.* Indianapolis, IN: New Riders.

Nickerson, R. S. (Ed.). (1995). *Emerging needs and opportunities for human factors research.* Washington, DC: National Academy of Sciences. Available at http://www.nap.edu/catalog/4940.html

Stanton, N. (1998). *Human factors in consumer products.* Bristol, PA: Taylor & Francis.

Wiklund, M. E. (1994). *Usability in practice: How companies develop user-friendly products.* San Francisco: Morgan Kaufmann.

Wolgalter, M. S., & Rogers, W. A. (1998). Human factors/ergonomics: Using psychology to make a better and safer world. *Eye on Psi Chi, 3*(1), 23–26. Available at http://www.psichi.org/content/publications/eye/volume/vol_3/3_1/wogalter.asp

WEB RESOURCES

Human Factors & Ergonomics Society
http://hfes.org/

International Institute for Environment and Development
http://www.iied.org/

Getting an Industrial Design Job
http://www.idsa.org/studentedu/GETIDJOB.html

Current Trends in Environmental Psychology
http://www.ucm.es/info/Psyap/iaap/evans.htm

Traveling in Cyberspace: Psychology of Software Design
http://siop.org/tip/backissues/TipJan00/11Craiger.htm

Product Development and Management Association
http://www.pdma.org/

Webword Usability Weblog
http://webword.com

Usability Special Interest Group: Salary and Career Information
http://www.stcsig.org/usability/topics/salary.html

PROFILE: RUSS BRANAGHAN, PH.D., FITCH, INC. (SOURCE: AMMODT, 2004)

I work for Fitch, Inc., an international design firm located in Worthington, Ohio. It is my job to make products more user friendly.

Just a few short years ago, the lion's share of the high technology market went to the product with the most features, lowest price, and slickest appearance. As consumers have become more technologically savvy, usability has risen as one of the technology's most important issues. Now, product review articles dedicate about 30% to their text to usability issues. Usable products share five characteristics.

1. Learnability: Usable products enable the user to get up to speed and accomplish meaningful work in a relatively short period of time.
2. Efficiency: Efficiency refers to the ease with which users perform their work once they have learned the system.
3. Memorability: What happens when users take a long break from using the product? When they return to it, do they remember how it works, or must they relearn it?
4. Error Minimization: The product should be designed so that the users make few errors and all errors should be easy to recover from.
5. Satisfaction: How pleasurable is the product to use? Users should feel productive, entertained, or satisfied after using it. Satisfaction is perhaps the most important usability factor in the commercial sense.

Usability is accomplished by ensuring the design fits the user rather than forcing the user to fit the design. This is accomplished by adhering to three principles:

1. Focus on the users, their tasks, and their environments.
2. Measure ease of use by scientific observational methods.
3. Improve the design in an iterative manner, making changes until users can easily and satisfactorily perform their tasks.

A good grasp of psychology is needed because successful design requires an understanding of the user's learning, memory, and judgment capabilities. Further, experimental design and analysis skills are needed to conduct usability tests. In these tests, users conduct realistic tasks with a prototype of the product while the researcher records whether the user was successful at the task, how long it took him or her to complete the task, and problems and design issues experienced along the way. The following case study illustrates how Finch, Inc. employs usability techniques to improve its clients' products.

Case Study: Teledyne Brown Engineering

Teledyne Brown asked Fitch to work on the design of an aircraft loader for the Air Force. The challenge was to design an interior for the cab that would enable the user to operate the vehicle safely, comfortably, and efficiently. The overall size and components of the cab were predetermined. Fitch assembled a team of designers, cognitive psychologists, and ergonomists to conduct field research to determine how users operate the current equipment, the difficulties they had, and what they liked and disliked about the product.

The field research showed that although aircraft loaders are currently designed to be operated while one is looking out through the front window (like an automobile or truck), operators actually lean their upper body out of the right side of the window 70% of the time to monitor the loads and communicate with people on the cargo deck. This made it difficult for operators to keep their eyes on the cargo and the airplane.

On the basis of this research, Fitch built a ìVelcroî model of the interior of the cab. Fake knobs, dials, and controls were attached so that they could be moved anywhere in the cab depending on the user's input. This enabled the team to work on the model itself rather than relying on drawings for design. The usability research provided invaluable feedback from the users. For example, one user relocated two controls so that a frequently performed operation that had previously required two hands could now be done with one. Further, the users suggested a slanted wall and raised seat that made it easier for operators to lean out of the cab and greatly enhanced visibility. The participatory, user-oriented approach allowed users, designers, and engineers to work together throughout the design process. The result was a smooth and rapid development of a superior product.

PROFILE: ROBERT R. TYLER, PH.D., CROWN CONSULTING, INC. (SOURCE: PSYCHOLOGICAL SCIENCE AGENDA, 2001)

While it is true that I was "doing" human factors long before I knew what it was, and certainly before I was designated a human factors practitioner, let's begin by understanding that I did not plan to have a career in Human Factors Psychology. I was an unsettled physics major during an unsettled time (the mid-sixties) who found himself midway through college learning to become a combat helicopter pilot. It was in a hostile foreign land that I learned first-hand the importance of good user-centered design processes. The aircraft that I flew in Vietnam was new, capable, and ostensibly designed to accomplish our combat mission. However, none of the operational procedures said anything as to how we would actually modify the prescribed flight profiles to get into and out of "hot" landing zones. Survival dictated that we minimize the time spent in slow and predictable flight trajectories.

So we abused the automation and modified the procedures by intentionally selecting in-flight rotor reprogramming positions—essentially creating two 52-diameter speedbrakes. We loved it until the back ends of the helicopters began falling off. The engineering solution: put in a speed sensor switch that prevents programming the rotors to the aft settings above 70 knots. The combat pilot's work-around: put your hand out the window and place it over the speed sensor to fool the system into believing it is below 70 knots. One additional glitch, the designers placed an identical switch next to the rotor trim switch that controlled the aircraft's stabilization system. Two clicks to the right of the rotor trim switch reprogrammed the rotors; two clicks either way of the stab-aug switch turned it off and caused the back end to want to swap places with the front end, thus guaranteeing real excitement when you least needed it!

Years later with an aviation safety degree in hand, I found myself buying and modifying venerable transport aircraft. As I sought to import technology into this 1950s airframe, issues of real estate, integration, and user habits/expectations surfaced. Most notable was an airborne navigator lament over the nonglare surface of his new color radar display. It seems he couldn't erase the grease pencil marks that he put on the screen during the conduct of rendezvous, despite the fact that the system was designed with all of the electronic "bells and whistles" to perform that function without the use of a grease pencil.

As a U.S. Marine Corps Naval Aviator, I was directly concerned with pilot error and aviation safety issues for over 30 years. At times I was part of the problem (as in the first example), and other times I sought to be part of the solution. As an instructor pilot, simulator instructor, and training squadron commander, I was where the "rubber meets the runway" on developing new pilots' skills in situational awareness, cockpit resource management, and aeronautical decision making while teaching them the basic stick and rudder skills. In my role as an acquisition executive, it was my goal to acquire training devices, aircraft systems, and decision support tools that enhanced the pilots' ability to understand their immediate flight environment.

I have watched the human factors discipline evolve as an applied science within aviation. At first, human factors was about fitting humans into specific cockpits. Later we began to focus on those "life stressors" that could distract a pilot and ultimately cause a mishap. The infusion of Total Quality Management and airlines' Cockpit Resource Management Principles into military flight operations continued to fuel the evolution toward a user-centered environment. Nonetheless, the issue of pilot error remained. As the Marine Corps' aviation safety director, I noted that during Desert Shield/Storm, once again, more aircraft crashed avoiding suspected enemy fire than were shot down. As I reviewed mishap reports and sat on boards determining aviators suitability for continued flight duties, I was increasingly plagued with the conundrum of why highly trained, physically fit, well-disciplined aviators would end up flying their superbly maintained, perfectly functioning, state-of-the-art flying machines into the ground. In search of answers to this question I found myself enrolled in a terminal degree program in Human Factors Psychology.

I have seen the effects of poor design. I have been exposed to a variety of aircraft and flight domains. I have observed good and bad aviation safety practices, and I was fortunate enough to be in positions where I could introduce procedures and methodologies that created safer flight environments. Clearly it has been an exciting, fulfilling, and circuitous route to this point in my career—one that I could not have charted or anticipated. Currently, I am an adjunct professor in Embry-Riddle's extended campus program and a human factors consultant to the Federal Aviation Administration. In both capacities, I continue to explore the challenges associated with infusing consideration of human capabilities and limitations into aviation environments.

Source: Tyler, R. R. (September/October 2000). An Interesting Career in Psychology: Aviation Human Factors Practitioner. Psychological Science Agenda (available at http://www.apa.org/science/ic-tyler.html)

ACADEMIA AND RESEARCH

CHAPTER GUIDE

Of all the careers described within this book, you're probably most familiar with that of the academic: careers as professors and researchers. However, you may be surprised at the wide range of academic careers available to industrial/organizational and human factors psychologists. Within this chapter, we'll explore the roles of work psychologists in academic and research settings.

A CAREER AS A PROFESSOR

Psychologists who work as professors are able to study and work with the information that they love—and share it with students. Industrial, organizational, and human factors psychologists are professors in a variety of academic departments. You can find work psychologists within psychology departments, business schools, schools of engineering, and many other places where you may have never expected psychologists to work.

Types of Academic Institutions

Academic careers as professors are similar in that all entail teaching and research; however, the balance among the two, or the relative amounts of teaching and research expected, varies by institution. There are several types of academic institutions and each holds differing expectations for faculty work. For example, community colleges tend to focus heavily on teaching. Professors usually teach five classes per semester and therefore focus most of their creative energy on teaching and usually conduct little research. Liberal arts colleges are small, highly selective colleges that emphasize quality instruction and lots of student-professor contact. Professors who work in liberal arts colleges are expected to be excellent teachers and to incorporate students into their research, meaning that they are expected to get students involved in their research and to help students conduct their own research. Usually professors in liberal arts colleges have heavy teaching and student contact requirements that limit the amount of research that they can conduct, so some, but not a lot of, research is expected of such professors.

At the other extreme are research universities. Research universities are large educational institutions with prestigious graduate programs. Professors who work at research institutions usually teach only one or two courses per semester and are expected to spend a large part of their time conducting research in their discipline. Unlike community and liberal arts colleges, in research institutions, performance evaluations, tenure (which we'll talk about in more depth later in this chapter), and promotions are based more heavily on research and scholarly publications than on teaching. Many four-year colleges and universities fall somewhere between the two extremes and encourage faculty to engage in both teaching and research. So, even within academia, there are several career tracks for work psychologists.

A Professor's Work

Regardless of a professor's institution, certain features hold true: all engage in some teaching, research, and community service activities, but in differing ratios, depending on the institution. There is much more to teaching than lecturing in front of a classroom. Before a professor steps into the classroom, several hours have gone into preparation because each day requires background reading of chapters and journal articles in addition to the textbook, note taking, and preparation of overheads, PowerPoint presentations, discussion questions, activities, and assignments. Preparation is never finished because the field is constantly changing and professors need to keep abreast of current trends and research in their fields. Professors who teach three or more classes per semester may find that preparation takes all of their time, especially early in their careers (Roediger, 1997). Outside of class, professors spend time grading papers, creating tests, scouring the library for current research to update their lectures, writing recommendation letters for students, holding office hours, and meeting with students to answer questions, advise them on decisions regarding their majors, careers, and courses.

In addition to teaching, most professors spend some of their time conducting research. Professors must divide their time among many tasks during a typical week, like writing an article or book chapter, planning research, analyzing research data, writing grant proposals to fund research, searching the literature, reading research articles, advising students on their research, and preparing or giving talks at professional meetings. Professors are often asked to review and provide expert feedback on articles submitted to professional journals as well as grants submitted to funding agencies.

Professors also engage in service activities at their universities. They participate in faculty meetings and sit on committees that help to structure and run the college or university. Many faculty also engage in service activities within the community surrounding the university. For example, some might serve as voluntary (i.e., pro bono) advisors for community agencies. Industrial or organizational psychologists might help social service agencies in hiring and evaluating employees, improving management, or assessing program outcomes (i.e., devising and carrying out methods to determine whether a prevention or intervention program works). Some professors also engage in consulting work in social service agencies, businesses, government agencies, and industries where they conduct research (as described later in this chapter), and assist in resolving personnel and organizational issues.

Advantages and Disadvantages to a Career as a Professor

A career as a professor has many advantages, but perhaps the best is the autonomy and flexibility of academic life. Professors are autonomous in the sense that they have academic freedom or are intellectually free; they may conduct whatever research strikes their fancy and, as Vesilind (2000) describes, they may "teach the truth as they see it" (p. 10). In other words, professors research problems that they see as fit to study and decide on the best methods to teach their courses. Textbooks, reading assignments, class activities, grading, and evaluation procedures are often up to the professor. Flexibility extends not only to professors' research and activities within the classroom, but also to their schedules. Aside from class time and committee meetings, professors' schedules tend to be adaptable. Most develop work habits that fit their lives, allowing time to pick up children from school, spend time with their families, and complete preparation and writing in the late evenings or early mornings.

Another advantage of a career as a professor is tenure. What is tenure? It's protection in the form of job security. Tenure provides complete academic freedom because it prevents professors from being fired for airing unpopular views or pursuing controversial research. Professors with documented teaching histories, excellent student evaluations, publications, campus committee work, and outreach to the community earn tenure and cannot be fired for airing unpopular views or researching controversial topics. Tenure ensures academic freedom because faculty can be free to teach and research the topics that interest them without fear. Other benefits of a career as a professor are intangible, such as the excitement of discovery and innovation, as well as the rewards of imparting knowledge and introducing students to a life of the mind (Roediger, 1997; Vesilind, 2000).

A career as a professor also entails disadvantages, most notably in securing a position to begin with. Academic positions are scarce—the job market is very competitive because there aren't a lot of positions available. Some applicants spend several years on the job market, working as postdoctoral researchers, in one-year instructor appointments, or adjunct positions (teaching part time, often at several colleges at once). Applicants must be prepared to seek faculty positions in a variety of geographic locations and cannot limit themselves to searching in only one place.

Once a position is obtained, new professors juggle many demands. In addition to teaching loads and service responsibilities, most new faculty are expected to begin a research program because in recent years research has increased in importance as well—even for those in "teaching" colleges (Salzinger, 1995). Faculty in research universities experience pressure to win large competitive research grants and publish in the best journals. Finally, as shown in Table 5.1, professors' salaries allow them to live comfortably, but certainly will not make them rich; however, professors who teach in business and engineering schools often earn salaries about 25% higher than other professors (Vroom, 1997).

TABLE 5.1	MEAN SALARIES FOR PROFESSORS

Institution and Position	Average Salary
Doctoral Institutions	
Professor	$97,910
Associate Professor	$67,043
Assistant Professor	$57,131
Comprehensive Institutions (Master's Level)	
Professor	$75,334
Associate professor	$59,326
Assistant professor	$48,965
Baccalaureate Institutions	
Professor	$69,598
Associate professor	$53,575
Assistant professor	$44,700

Adapted from Chronicle of Higher Education, 2003

Training and Preparation for a Career as a Professor

A graduate degree is needed to become a college professor. With a master's degree you can teach undergraduate students part time as an adjunct instructor, or full time within a 2-year or community college. However, faculty positions at community colleges have become more competitive in recent years and many are held by psychologists with doctoral degrees (Lloyd, 2000; Peters, 1992). If your goal is to become a college professor, seek a doctoral degree because it will provide you with the most opportunities for employment, mobility, and advancement as a faculty member.

Getting into a doctoral program isn't enough to ensure that you'll be competitive or well prepared for a faculty position after you graduate. While attending graduate school, seek research and teaching experiences that will prepare you for a career as a professor. Get involved in research early in your graduate school career, which is relatively easy to do given that doctoral programs tend to emphasize research. However, in addition to assisting your advisor or supervisor with his or her research, you must develop a research program of your own. Given that the purpose of doctoral study is to become an independent researcher, this task isn't out of the ordinary. In addition to be competitive for faculty positions, you must also publish your research in the best scholarly journals possible and present it at national and regional professional meetings. Your graduate school advisor can help you to develop and hone these research skills. Many students seek additional training in research after completing their doctorates in psychology; they become postdoctoral fellows who are paid to conduct research and become apprentices to major researchers in their fields of study. A postdoctoral fellowship will buy you additional time to conduct research and get the publications needed to be an attractive job candidate.

Although doctoral students receive ample training in research, few obtain training in teaching. Professors must be familiar with pedagogy, or the art of teaching, yet few doctoral programs provide this sort of training (Kuther, 2002; 2003a). Successful professors master the techniques of their trade and learn to compose lectures, lead discussions, create syllabi, and enhance student learning through the effective use of the blackboard, overheads, or PowerPoint presentations. Good teachers—those who can make the course material come to life and interest students—aren't born, they're made. It takes a great deal of practice, work, and effort to teach well; unfortunately few graduate students learn this secret.

If you're interested in becoming a professor, seek a graduate program that helps to prepare students for the teaching aspects of the professorate. Many graduate programs have seminars and courses in how to teach. The Preparing Future Faculty program, a program designed to prepare aspiring academics for the variety of teaching, research, and service roles entailed in the professorate, has also created a wealth of resources and a website available at http://www.preparing-faculty.org/ (American Psychological Association, 2001; Preparing Future Faculty, n.d.). During graduate school, seek practical experience as a teaching assistant or adjunct professor at your university or a nearby college. You can also volunteer to teach a class or two for your primary instructors or for instructors teaching courses in your area of interest. Most importantly, find a mentor in graduate school who can help you with these essential aspects of training so that your students aren't guinea pigs for your first experiments in teaching (Kuther, 2002, in press).

A CAREER IN RESEARCH

Industrial, organizational, and human factors psychologists also pursue careers in research conducting basic and applied studies of human behavior. They study factors that lead to eye fatigue, the influence of temperature on productivity, group dynamics and leadership, employee motivation, and many other topics. You'll find work psychologists in a variety of research settings including universities, government agencies, private organizations, military settings, and in businesses and corporations. Let's take a closer look at the many settings in which you can find research psychologists who specialize in industrial, organizational, and human factors psychology.

Academia

Many psychologists work in university settings as scientists, conducting basic and applied research. For example, an industrial psychologist might design a measure to assess work-related skills. Another work psychologist might design a research program to examine personality characteristics common to effective leaders, explore how leaders influence organizations, and understand how communication strategies influence how a leader's message is interpreted. A human factors psychologist might conduct basic research on the eye's reactivity to light, as well as applied research on how to modify computer screens to reduce glare and eyestrain.

A research career in academia offers a flexible schedule and is prestigious. Research scientists gain independence and autonomy as they progress in their careers. By writing and winning research grants, research scientists are able to fund their own research and choose what problems they study. With advancement, research scientists take on supervisory roles, run their own labs, and train graduate students and postdoctoral students. Researchers have many opportunities for travel through speaking at conferences. They also may come into contact with the public through consulting and writing for the popular press (Bartholomew, 2001a).

A disadvantage of a research career in academia is the competition. Generally, academic positions that don't require teaching can be difficult to obtain. Applicants may need to be geographically mobile and able to relocate for available positions. Research and professorial careers in academia entail long hours because academics must "publish or perish." Publish or perish is just that: publish many articles in prestigious journals, or lose your job! As you might imagine, this can be very stressful for professors. Research and publication are tenuous and lengthy processes, as new professors may spend many evenings in the lab, carrying out research, or at the computer, analyzing data or writing articles for publication. Successfully publishing your research, however, is very rewarding and enables you to contribute to your field.

Industry

Industrial, organizational, and human factors psychologists are plentiful in business and industry settings. Psychologists in business conduct surveys of consumer opinion, for example, and study ways of improving employee productivity. Psychologists who work as researchers in industry settings study many of the same problems as do those in academia. Organizational psychologists might study the management structure of various organizations to determine the most efficient configuration of managers. A human factors psychologist might design a car's dashboard to allow drivers the ability to easily see and reach the displays and knobs while viewing the road. Another psychologist might study how consumers scan store shelves when they look for products and what types of packaging attracts consumers' attention.

A career in industry is different from academia because in industry, the focus is on promoting the success of the company. The goal is to create products and increase productivity to benefit the company, employees, and shareholders (Bartholomew, 2001b). Research takes place at a faster pace in industry than in academia because information must be gathered quickly to help create and sell products. Teams conduct the research, enabling greater productivity. In addition, psychologists in business and industry settings tend to have access to more funding than do those in academia, meaning that they tend to work with newer and more sophisticated equipment. The primary drawback of conducting research in business and industry is that your research questions are assigned based on the needs of the company, not necessarily on your interests. An important benefit of working in industry is the contact with people of diverse fields and educational backgrounds. You may have the opportunity to conduct research in fields that are outside of your immediate discipline as industry needs are often vast, so you'll be able to apply the scientific method to a variety of problems that you may not have encountered in academia. Other benefits are the high salaries and regular work schedule; in business and industry, your weekends generally are your own.

Government and Military

Although research psychologists engage in similar activities regardless of work setting, whether universities, industry, or government/military, the three settings differ in terms of the autonomy afforded researchers. Similar to researchers in industry, those employed by the government and military (as nonenlisted contractors) usually examine research questions not conceived by them (Herrman, 1997). Instead, researchers in government and military settings examine questions that are created by politicians, policy makers, and defense strategists designed to promote the security and well-being of the American people. Your work will have the potential to affect many people over a long period of time, and thus, research questions are often more complex and require collaboration with many other government researchers and agencies (Copper, 1997).

An advantage of a research career in government and the military is that you'll be exposed to many different projects. Unlike academia, where researchers spend a career focused on a particular research problem or area, research psychologists in government work on a diverse range of projects and become generalists. Most research projects initiated by the government are short in duration (about 1 year to complete) because the research is intended to help resolve practical problems. Also, shifts in public opinion and interest lead political leaders to eliminate some projects and initiate new ones. Of course, whether this is an advantage or disadvantage depends on your interest in the project. If you're interested in a research career in government or the military, be prepared to engage in lots of supervisory work because contractors conduct much of the hands-on work, under supervision by government researchers. This enables government researchers to work on multiple projects at once and not become overly involved in any one project. Like industry, government and military research involves working on a team because the government is interested in applied research topics, requiring creativity and planning by an interdisciplinary team of researchers consisting of psychologists, sociologists, statisticians, computer scientists, economists, and more.

Social Service Agencies and Nonprofits

Research psychologists employed at social service or nonprofit agencies conduct research to assess and improve the agency's programs and often write grants to help fund the agency. Social service and nonprofit agencies often are contracted by the government to conduct policy analyses, literature reviews, and research to improve decision making by political leaders and consumers. A psychologist at such an agency might examine the effectiveness of highway safety initiatives or antiterrorism strategies at an airport.

The primary benefit of working in a nonprofit or social service agency is that your time is focused on research that may lead to social change rather than teaching or academic curriculum meetings. Such agencies tend to conduct interdisciplinary research, enabling research psychologists to work with a diverse range of specialists of other fields. Though the salaries at nonprofit and social service agencies tend to be lower than in other research settings, the research often directly benefits consumers and families.

Careers in Research: Preparation and Salary

While bachelor's-degree holders often can become research assistants, graduate degrees offer more opportunities for advancement. Many research positions are available to master's-degree holders, especially in industry, government, and nonprofit and social service agencies. In academic settings, the doctoral degree offers the most flexibility, opportunities for advancement, and opportunities to serve as the primary investigator of federal grants (Lloyd, 2000). Research psychologists in academia often obtain 2 to 3 years of postdoctoral training after obtaining the doctoral degree. As shown in Table 5.2, salaries for research positions vary by setting.

| TABLE 5.2 | MEDIAN SALARIES FOR DOCTORAL-LEVEL CAREERS IN RESEARCH (WITH 2–4 YEARS' EXPERIENCE) |

Median Salary	
University research center	$45,000
Private research organization	$57,000
Government research organization	$57,000
Nonprofit organization	$61,532
Industry	$78,824

Adapted from Singleton, Tate, & Randall, 2003; Williams, Wicherski, & Kohout, 2000, and adjusted for 2003.

CAREERS IN THE MILITARY

In addition to a career as nonenlisted researchers, some work psychologists enlist in the military. The military offers may opportunities for work psychologists, including roles in personnel selection and classification, training, human factors, and leadership and team effectiveness (American Psychological Association, n.d., Wisckoff, 1997).

Activities of Psychologists in the Military

Some psychologists in the military engage in personnel selection and classification. They screen, select, and place recruits, and select personnel for jobs requiring special skills such as piloting aircraft, air traffic control, and special operations personnel. They create procedures for evaluating the performance of enlisted and officer personnel and conduct research on how to use simulators to evaluate special abilities. Psychologists in the military also train personnel. They conduct research examining the most effective techniques for training personnel in basic skills, military skills, and technical skills, as well as how to increase operational readiness. They conduct research on how to design effective instructional systems, measure training performance, and best use computer-simulated scenarios and technology such as virtual reality.

Other psychologists in the military work in human factors and engineering to design the human-machine interfaces that improve the functioning of military systems and equipment. For example, how can artificial intelligence and the use of sophisticated computer systems enhance human decision making? Psychologists study how to help military personnel operate most efficiently, maintain health, enhance performance, and reduce human error under adverse circumstances, such as without sleep, in extreme environmental conditions, and under hazardous conditions. Human factors psychologists in the military study how to develop and modify equipment to enhance performance. For example, a psychologist might study how night vision goggles can help pilots who fly at night: What are the advantages and disadvantages of pilots' use of night goggles? How can night goggles be modified to enhance contrast sensitivity, visual acuity, target detection, and motion detection, thereby aiding pilots and improving their safety and effectiveness?

Some psychologists study team effectiveness and how to improve communication in multinational forces. Psychologists study how to promote effective leadership as well as how to select, train, and evaluate leaders. Some might get involved in political-psychological issues such as study of the behavior of world leaders. Others examine team processes such as structure, communication, subordinate-supervisor relations, team cohesion, the functioning of small groups, and tactical decision making.

Military Career: Advantages, Disadvantages, and Salary

Psychologists in the military often spend significant amounts of time overseas, which, depending on your inclination and family situation, may be an advantage or disadvantage. A uniformed psychologist can count on a change of geographical location every 2 to 3 years (Wiskoff, 1997). As a psychologist in the military, you'll have the opportunity to see the world.

A final potential limitation for psychologists in the military is the issue of enlistment. Unlike other psychology positions, working for the military isn't optional once you join the ranks—you'll become an officer and must serve for the duration of your commitment. Psychologists in academia, business and industry, or other branches of the government have the option of leaving their job if they decide they no longer want to do it, but military psychologists don't have this option. Consider your own level of satisfaction and comfort with the military lifestyle because once you're sworn in as an officer, you can't change your mind and simply go do something else. Other important benefits of military service include job security, opportunities for additional education, and an excellent benefits and retirement system. Few professional positions offer the opportunity to retire after as few as twenty years of service, and to do so with a pension. The salary scale for military psychologists is aligned with the government pay scales (Wiskoff, 1997). In 2001, government starting salary for master's-level psychologists was $33,300; starting salary for doctoral-level psychologists was $40,200 (Bureau of Labor Statistics, 2002).

SUGGESTED READINGS

Goldberg, J. (1996). *Opportunities in research and development careers.* New York: McGraw-Hill.

Sternberg, R. J. (1997). *Career paths in psychology: Where your degree can take you.* Washington, DC: American Psychological Association.

Vesilind, P. A. (2000). *So you want to be a professor? A handbook for graduate students.* Thousand Oaks, CA: Sage.

WEB RESOURCES

Career Path Less Traveled
  http://www.apa.org/monitor/feb01/careerpath.html

Council of Teachers of Undergrad Psychology
  http://newton.uor.edu/facultyfolder/rickabaugh/ctup/ctup.html

Society for the Teaching of Psychology
  http://teachpsych.lemoyne.edu/

Office of Teaching Resources in Psychology
  http://www.lemoyne.edu/OTRP/index.html

Preparing Future Faculty
  http://www.preparing-faculty.org/

Military Career Guide Online
  http://www.militarycareers.com/

About the U.S. Military
  http://usmilitary.about.com/

Career Development Center for Postdocs and Junior Faculty
  http://nextwave.sciencemag.org/feature/careercenter.shtml

Military Career Advice
  http://www.learnatest.com/military/careeradvice/index.cfm

Science, Math, and Engineering Career Resources
  http://www.Ph.D.s.org/

PROFILE: SUSAN A. FERGUSON, PH.D., INSURANCE INSTITUTE FOR HIGHWAY SAFETY (SOURCE: PSYCHOLOGICAL SCIENCE AGENDA, 1997)

Like many other... graduate students, I began graduate school with the intention of pursuing a traditional career in academe. I had a strong interest in research and a love of learning that I thought would carry over into teaching. But after many years in graduate school and a number of opportunities spanning about 5 years teaching psychology to undergraduates, I realized that the academic life was not for me. Research was what I wanted to do—preferably in a field that would offer variety and challenge.

With an open mind, I interviewed for a position as a research analyst with the Insurance Institute for Highway Safety. I knew nothing about highway safety, but had all the right skills to conduct research, even though my skills were honed in a predominantly experimental setting. I met with a multidisciplinary team of researchers at the Institute, including other psychologists, statisticians, epidemiologists, and engineers, all of whom brought different and complementary skills to the field. This was the perfect research setting for me to focus on producing high-quality research among a team of professionals. When the position was offered to me, I accepted with a clear heart, but not without the usual trepidation that accompanies a major career shift.

Since that first day in my new job over 5 years ago, there has never been a dull moment. As is necessary for all research, to conduct highway safety research, one must be able to design studies applying basic scientific principles, to supervise research, analyze data, draw conclusions, and write reports. In this case, however, the domain of interest was the real world of highway safety, so as a researcher, I had to mesh experimental design principles with practical reality. The variety of research in which the Institute is involved also provided an exciting new challenge for me. The mission of the Institute is to find ways to reduce the losses on our nation's highways—losses due to injury, death, and property damage. What this means in practice is that everything that has a direct impact on motor vehicle safety is up for grabs. William Haddon, the first administrator of the National Highway Traffic Safety Administration (then called National Highway Safety Bureau) and the Institute's founder, espoused many years ago that there are several ways to improve highway safety. He proposed that countermeasures should target pre-crash events, the crash itself, and post-crash events. Within each of these phases, there are human, vehicle, and environmental factors that can be targeted. Putting these crash phases and factors together yields a practical and multifaceted approach for reducing highway losses.

In the last 5 years, I have conducted research on many different topics, including teenage driving, alcohol-impaired driving, daylight saving time effects, and occupant restraint systems. I have published this work in many peer-reviewed journals and have presented my results at a variety of forums including to the local community, the highway safety community, and federal and state legislators. This diversity has required the wearing of many different hats and at least a working knowledge of other disciplines such as epidemiology, engineering, and physics. But perhaps the most rewarding aspect of this job is the opportunity to educate and inform many groups of stakeholders, from consumers to state and federal institutions. For example, Institute research is used by the federal government to inform the regulatory process governing vehicle safety standards, and at the state level, to design laws governing driver behavior. We also provide consumer-oriented materials, both written materials and videotapes, on subjects such as vehicle crashworthiness, teenage driving, and airbag safety, which can help consumers decide what vehicles to buy, how to reduce risks for beginning drivers, and how to avoid airbag-related injuries. A big part of the Institute's job is to inform the community about important highway-safety issues and countermeasures that can really make a difference. To this end, we provide media outlets with the results of our research and keep them informed about the emerging issues that they should cover.

What this all adds up to is a job that is full of variety and challenge. It requires an ability to handle multiple projects and to respond to emerging priorities. If you are looking for a field where your research can really make a difference, perhaps you should consider highway safety research.

Source: Susan A. Ferguson, PhD (January/February 1997). An Interesting Career in Psychology: Highway Safety Research Analyst. Psychological Science Agenda (available at http://www.apa.org/science/ic-ferguson.html)

PROFILE: DEBORAH L. GEBHARDT, PH.D., HUMAN PERFORMANCE SYSTEMS, INC. (SOURCE: AMMODT, 2004)

My company conducts research to develop and validate physical performance and cognitive tests and medical guidelines. To provide our clients with valid, defensible selection, evaluation, and promotion instruments, we conduct detailed job analyses to determine job requirements. Job analysis provides the foundation for establishing the validity of selection and promotion procedures. To develop valid, defensible procedures that reflect the essential job functions, the job tasks, knowledges, skills, and abilities must be defined. Conducting the job analysis can be one of the most rewarding aspects of a project because the job analyst is exposed to new environments and new people.

To be an effective job analyst, one must be able to learn the details involved in another person's job. This is a highlight of the process because it affords us the opportunity to visit job sites and interview incumbents. These site visits have provided us with some exciting and interesting experiences. For example, our work in the natural gas industry involved observing work performed on a drilling platform 100 miles out in the Gulf of Mexico to learn how to repair engines with five-foot-long pistons. Similarly, interviewing workers in a man-hole while they repair telephone cable provides a true understanding of why there may be occasional static in your home phone line.

Each project provides new challenges to the job analyst in capturing the purpose and details associated with the job tasks. In many instances, this information is best obtained by accompanying the worker on a shift and participating in the work. To understand the work of public safety personnel, we rode with paramedics in New York City, followed firefighters into a burning building, and answered dispute calls with police officers.

When developing physical performance assessment procedures and medical guidelines, it is important to gather information about the ergonomic parameters that affect the work place and the worker. Ergonomics applies knowledge of human capabilities and requirements to the design of work devices, systems, and the physical work setting. Ergonomic evaluations can involve specific analysis of working postures and their effect on muscle fatigue or general gathering of data such as heights, weights, and forces involved in task performance. This again involves on-site measurements and observations. For instance, we obtained measurements of the forces required to open the hatches and doors on navy destroyers and in nuclear power plants. In another study, learning to climb telephone poles was necessary to obtain the ergonomic data needed to determine whether men and women used different climbing techniques.

Conducting a job analysis provides an appreciation and understanding for the ingenuity of the American workforce. We observed firsthand the advances in mechanized and electronic control systems and administrative procedures that have increased productivity, made work environments more pleasant, and decreased work-related injuries.

The key to performing an accurate job analysis is to get involved in the process by learning as much as possible about the job. All jobs are not exciting, but for a job analyst it is important to be interested in the job and allow the incumbent to provide relevant information. This requires asking many questions about the work to obtain detailed information. To do this effectively, the job analyst must be fully and genuinely engaged in the process.

IS INDUSTRIAL-ORGANIZATIONAL PSYCHOLOGY OR HUMAN FACTORS FOR YOU?

CHAPTER

6

CHAPTER GUIDE

Throughout this book we've explored various career paths in the fields known as work psychology. In this chapter, we extend our discussion to education and training in industrial, organizational, and human factors psychology: How do you get to where you'd like to be, careerwise? We'll discuss master's degrees and doctoral degrees, the paths to a career in work psychology, and what you can do now, as an undergraduate, to prepare for your career.

GRADUATE STUDY IN WORK PSYCHOLOGY

While there are some entry-level positions for bachelor's-degree holders, a graduate degree is required for a career in industrial, organizational, or human factors psychology. If you're considering graduate study in work psychology, do some research and learn about the various degree options available to you.

Master's Degrees

Your advisor is a good source of information about graduate study in general, but be sure to supplement his or her advice with your own research because advisors often know little about master's degrees in psychology (Actkinson, 2000), despite the fact that a far greater number of psychology students pursue master's degrees than doctoral degrees (Kuther, 2003a). Each year, about 13,000 students earn master's degrees in psychology (Hays-Thomas, 2000).

A master's degree typically requires 2 years of study beyond the bachelor's degree (sometimes compressed into 1 very busy year). There are many different types of master's degrees, but the most common are the M.A. (master of arts) and M.S. (master of science). Usually there is no substantive difference between an M.A. and an M.S. Although some universities or departments award only one or the other. Occasionally a psychology department may award both. In those instances, an M.A. may require a thesis and an M.S. may substitute additional statistics and research courses and a comprehensive exam for the thesis, but this is not always the case (Lloyd, 2000).

What does a master's degree entail? Similar to your undergraduate experience, you'll take many courses as a master's student. Because master's programs entail fewer credit hours than doctoral programs, they tend to have a more narrow focus on developing students' basic competencies (Society for Industrial and Organizational Psychology, 1994). Master's-level practitioners are trained to be consumers of the industrial/organizational psychology knowledge base and apply it to issues involving individuals and groups in organizational settings. Specifically, master's students in industrial and organizational psychology are trained in the following competencies (Society for Industrial and Organizational Psychology, 1994):

- Core Psychological Domains
  - History and Systems of Psychology
  - Fields of Psychology
- Data Collection and Analysis Skills
  - Research Methods
  - Statistical Methods/Data Analysis
  - Core Industrial-Organizational Domains
  - Ethical, Legal, and Professional Contexts
  - Measurement of Individual Differences
  - Criterion Theory and Development
  - Job and Task Analysis
  - Employee Selection, Placement, and Classification
  - Performance Appraisal and Feedback
  - Training: Theory, Program Design, and Evaluation
  - Work Motivation
  - Attitude Theory
  - Small Group Theory and Process
  - Organization Theory
  - Organizational Development

According to the Society for Industrial and Organizational Psychology (1994), all master's programs in industrial/organizational psychology should provide some training in each of the areas described as core psychological, data collection and analysis, and industrial/organizational competencies. Note that the training emphasizes breadth rather than depth to provide master's-level practitioners with background knowledge and methodological skills to make informed judgments on how to apply industrial/organizational knowledge to real-world settings. Training in additional competencies that are beneficial, but not essential, and not offered at all master's programs in industrial/organizational psychology include (Society for Industrial and Organizational Psychology, 1994):

- Career Development Theory
- Human Performance/Human Factors
- Consumer Behavior
- Compensation and Benefits
- Industrial and Labor Relations

Because master's programs entail approximately 30 credit hours, they do not include training in all aspects of industrial/organizational psychology. Given the narrow focus, there is a great deal of variability in training emphases among master's programs. In addition to coursework, many master's programs entail an internship or field experience in which students are placed in work settings and get hands-on supervised experience in the field. Before applying, thoroughly research curricula of master's programs as well as the range of field experiences to ensure that the training will be sufficient for your career goals.

Doctoral Degrees

A doctoral degree provides a greater range of flexibility than does a master's degree. A doctoral degree will prepare you for more advanced positions in industrial/organizational psychology, as well as research and academic positions. Typically, a doctoral degree requires 5 to 7 years of graduate work. Like master's degrees, pursing a doctoral degree will entail taking courses. According to the Society for Industrial and Organizational Psychology, doctoral programs should provide training in the following areas of competence (Society for Industrial and Organizational Psychology, 1999):

- Consulting and Business Skills
- Ethical, Legal, and Professional Skills
- Fields of Psychology
- History and Systems of Psychology
- Research Methods
- Statistical Methods and Data Analysis
- Attitude Theory, Measurement, and Change
- Career Development
- Consumer Behavior
- Criterion Theory and Development
- Health and Stress in Organizations
- Human Performance/Human Factors
- Individual Assessment
- Individual Differences
- Job Evaluation and Compensation
- Job/Task Analysis and Classification
- Judgment and Decision Making

- Leadership and Management
- Organization Development
- Organization Theory
- Performance Appraisal and Feedback
- Personnel Recruitment, Selection, and Placement
- Small Group Theory and Team Processes
- Training: Theory, Program Design, and Evaluation
- Work Motivation

Most doctoral programs offer applied experiences such as field work and internships that enable students to get hands-on experience under the supervision of an industrial/organizational psychologist. Not only are the curricula of doctoral programs more substantial than master's-level programs, but doctoral degrees also immerse students in research. While master's-level programs train students to be consumers of industrial/organizational knowledge, doctoral programs train students to create knowledge through the conduct of research.

The doctor of philosophy in psychology is a research degree that prepares graduates for a range of careers in research, university teaching, and practice. Most doctoral programs in industrial/organizational psychology follow the scientist-practitioner model of training, meaning that students are trained to be scientists, by conducting research, as well as practitioners. Research is emphasized in PhD programs; typically students engage in research with their advisors throughout the graduate program and then complete a dissertation based on their own original research. If you're considering earning a PhD, carefully consider the research emphases of the faculty members at each program to ensure that you'll have the opportunity and support to explore your interests and career goals. Examine the suggested readings and Web resources on applying to graduate school at the end of this chapter for in-depth advice on the process of applying to graduate school.

ADVANCING YOUR CAREER: WHAT YOU CAN DO NOW

So, you think that a career in industrial, organizational, or human factors psychology is for you. What can you do now, as an undergraduate, to prepare for such a career?

Take relevant undergraduate courses: Courses might include industrial/organizational psychology, human factors, statistics, research methods, computer programming, business, finance, accounting, social psychology, consumer psychology, cognitive psychology, personnel law, and psychological testing.

Seek research experience . Assist professors with their research or develop an independent research project. Research in industrial/organizational psychology may be especially useful, but any research experience will help you to grow as a scholar. Research experience demonstrates your ability to work independently, as well as your analytical and critical thinking skills. It's evidence of your motivation, initiative, and willingness to go beyond basic requirements.

Enhance your communication skills. Take courses in English, writing, and communications. Learn how to make effective oral and written presentations.

Get internship experience. Seek an undergraduate internship. There are many internship opportunities within business and industry settings. An internship or practicum will provide you with hands-on experience as well as the chance to sample a potential career and discover what work psychology is really about.

Remember that there are also a variety of psychology-related positions that you can obtain with your undergraduate degree. Consider getting work experience if you're not sure whether graduate school or work psychology is for you. Box 6.1 provides a list of positions for students who are interested in pursuing careers with undergraduate degree in psychology. As you can see, graduate education isn't always necessary to apply psychology to work settings. Of course, graduate education opens the doors to many different positions as well as to career advancement, but whether to pursue graduate education is your choice, depending on where it fits with your career goals, interests, and life. Take your time with this decision, explore your interests and options, and be true to yourself to find a career that you'll find rewarding and fulfilling.

BOX 6-1

INDUSTRIAL-ORGANIZATIONAL PSYCHOLOGY-RELATED POSITIONS FOR BACHELOR'S DEGREE GRADUATES IN PSYCHOLOGY

Administrative assistant
Affirmative action officer
Advertising trainee
Benefits manager
Career counselor
Claims specialist
Community relations officer
Customer relations
Data management
Employee recruitment
Employment counselor
Human resources coordinator/manager/specialist
Labor relations manager/specialist
Loan officer
Management trainee
Marketing
Occupational therapist
Personnel manager/officer
Product and services research
Programs/events coordination
Public relations
Retail sales management
Sales representative
Special features writing/reporting
Staff training and development
Trainer/Training officer

(Note that some positions require additional training. Source: Kuther, 2003a)

SUGGESTED READINGS

American Psychological Association. (1994). *Getting in: A step-by-step plan for gaining admission to graduate school in psychology.* Washington, DC: Author.

American Psychological Association (2002). *Graduate study in psychology: 2003 Edition.* Washington, DC: Author.

Bolles, R. N. (2000). *What color is your parachute? A practical manual for job-hunters and career-changers.* Berkeley, CA: Ten Speed Press.

Keith-Spiegel, P., & Wiederman, M. W. (2000). *Complete guide to graduate school admissions: Psychology, counseling, and related professions.* Mahwah, NJ: Erlbaum.

Kuther, T. L. (2003). *The psychology major's handbook.* Pacific Grove, CA: Wadsworth.

Kuther, T. L. (2004). *Getting into graduate school in psychology: Your guide to success.* Springfield, IL: Charles C. Thomas.

WEB RESOURCES

Applying to Graduate School
    http://www.psichi.org/content/publications/eye/category/grad_school.asp

Applying to Psychology Graduate Programs
    http://www.cas.okstate.edu/psych/undergrad/gradbook/ApplyGradProg.html

A Suggested Plan for Grad School Admission
    http://www.psynt.iupui.edu/undgrad/timeline.htm

About Graduate School
    http://gradschool.about.com

Graduate Training Programs in Industrial-Organizational Psychology and Related Fields
    http://siop.org/gtp/Default.htm

Trends and Issues in I-O Psychology:†A Glimpse into the Crystal Ball†
    http://siop.org/tip/backissues/TipApr01/09Harris.htm

The Licensing of I-O Psychologists
    http://siop.org/tip/backissues/TIPJan02/02licensing.htm

Pursing an I/O Psychology Career
    http://chuma.cas.usf.edu/~spector/pursuingio.html

Directory of Human Factors/Ergonomics Graduate Programs in the United States and Canada
    http://www.hfes.org/publications/2002gradschools/TofC.html

Quick Tips for Finding a Human Factors/Ergonomics Job in Industry
    http://www.hfes.org/publications/quicktips1.html

What's An I/O Job Like?
    http://chuma.cas.usf.edu/~spector/iojob.html

Who Are Industrial/Organizational (I/O) Psychologists?
    http://www.rci.rutgers.edu/~jraiello/IOpsych.htm

Psychology Alumni Careers
  http://www.gac.edu/oncampus/academics/psych/careers/FL_97.html

Graduate Training Programs in Industrial-Organizational Psychology and Related Fields
  http://www.siop.org/gtp/gtp98/gtp98toc.htm

Have you Considered Marketing or Organizational Behavior?
  http://www.geocities.com/Heartland/Flats/5353/classes/psychology.business.html

---

PROFILE: TEMEA SIMMONS, M.S., FEDERAL LABOR RELATIONS AUTHORITY (SOURCE: AMMODT, 2004)

I am a human resource trainee for the Federal Labor Relations Authority (FLRA), an independent agency responsible for directing the labor-management relations program for over 1.9 million non-postal federal employees. Our human resource division implements organizational policies and programs that enable FLRA's 210 employees to excel. I am one of the four personnel management specialists. My position is different from the other three specialists in that I am a trainee under a federal government training program known as the Outstanding Scholars Program. The Outstanding Scholars program provides college graduates with career-related employment that enriches their academic experience and offers valuable work experience in their chosen career.

Over a 2-year period, I will rotate through several different human resource areas such as compensation, performance management, and staffing. Such rotations are common in most management training programs. On the basis of my experiences, I believe that there are several questions you must ask yourself before entering a management or leadership training program.

Do you possess the necessary characteristics to retain and take advantage of each learning experience during your management training program? Characteristics I believe to be essential are self-motivation, confidence, adaptability, self-discipline, assertiveness, and creativity. These are important traits because you have to take the initiative and responsibility to make things happen for your individual career progression and performance goals. No one expects you to know what to do at all times, but you must be able to learn from your experiences.

Are your trainers capable and willing to train you? During the rotation of most management training programs, you are being supervised by a variety of individuals. With your desire to learn, would you not want to emulate or be influenced by the behavior of someone who has no leadership skills or lacks the motivation and enthusiasm to train you? It is additionally important that a well-established plan be developed that describes training outcomes and expectations. As a trainee, you should take responsibility for ensuring that your trainer provides you with the training set forth in the plan.

Will you be involved in decision making? As a trainee, it is sometimes difficult to participate in decision making. It is important however, to learn how decisions are made within an organization.

Does the organization have a career plan for you after you complete the program? If you feel that your training program was well planned and coordinated to provide you with the necessary experiences and training, you may want to continue employment there. Thus, it is important that the organization have a plan for your continued employment.

I believe that after graduating from college, management training programs should be considered. Exposure to management training programs prepares you for leadership roles and increases your marketability. My experience has proved to be very rewarding and beneficial. My initial salary was less than half of my counterparts, but it increases tremendously with each year of experience. You must be able to sacrifice the immediate need for a high salary by focusing on the wealth of knowledge, increased leadership skills, and magnitude of benefits that can be obtained through a well-structured management training program.

References

Aamodt, M. G. (2004). *Applied industrial/organizational psychology.* Pacific Grove, CA: Wadsworth.

Abbott, Langer, & Associates, Inc. (2001). *Compensation in the Publishing Field.* Retrieved May 20, 2003, from http://www.careerjournal.com/salaries/industries/media/20010913-publishing-tab.html

Actkinson, T. R. (2000). Master's and myth: Little-known information about a popular degree. *Eye on Psi Chi, 4*(2), 19–21, 23, 25.

American Institute of Graphic Arts. (2002). *Salary survey, 2002.* Retrieved May 20, 2003, from http://www.aiga.org/content.cfm?Alias=2000salarysurvey

American Psychological Association (n.d.). *Employed psychology PhDs by setting: 1997.* Retrieved July 20, 2001, from http://research.apa.org/doc10.html

American Psychological Association (2001). *Preparing future faculty program.* Retrieved January 18, 2002, from http://www.apa.org/ed/pff.html

Bartholomew, D. (2001a). Academia or industry: Finding the fit. *Next Wave.* Retrieved February 1, 2002, from http://nextwave.sciencemag.org/cgi/content/full/2000/08/10/6

Bartholomew, D. (2001b). Academia or industry: Where would I fit in? *Next Wave.* Retrieved February 1, 2002, from http://nextwave.sciencemag.org/cgi/content/full/2000/06/15/1

Bureau of Labor Statistics (2002). *Occupational outlook handbook.* Retrieved May 20, 2003, from http://stats.bls.gov/oco/ocoiab.htm

Careers in Business (2000). *Careers in business.* Retrieved June 5, 2002, from http://www.careers-in-business.com

Careerjournal.com. (n.d.). *Management-Consulting-Company Professionals Average annual total compensation.* Retrieved February 1, 2004, from: http://www.careerjournal.com/salaryhiring/industries/consulting/20040130-manage-consult-tab.html

Chronicle of Higher Education. (2003). *What professors earn.* Retrieved June 18, 2003, from http://chronicle.com/weekly/v49/i32/32a01501.htm

Clay, R. A. (2000). Often, the bells and whistles backfire. *Monitor on Psychology.* Retrieved June 5, 2002, from http://www.apa.org/monitor/apr00/usability.html

Cohen, J. (2002). I/Os in the know offer insights on Generation X workers. *Monitor on Psychology.* Retrieved November 8, 2003, from http://www.apa.org/monitor/feb02/genxwork.html

Conaway, A. (2000). *Careers in environmental psychology.* Retrieved May 20, 2003, from http://www.wcupa.edu/_ACADEMICS/sch_cas.psy/Career_Paths/Environmental/career09.htm

Copper, C. (1997). An interesting career in psychology: Social science analyst in the public sector. *Psychological Science Agenda.* Retrieved January 19, 2002, from http://www.apa.org/science/ic-copper.html

Day, M. C. (1996). An interesting career in psychology: Human-computer interface designer. *Psychological Science Agenda.* Retrieved May 20, 2003, from http://www.apa.org/science/ic-day.html

Fabris, P. (1998). *Data mining: Advanced navigation.* Retrieved June 16, 2002 from http://www.cio.com/archive/051598_mining.html

Foxhall, K. (2002). More psychologists are attracted to the executive coaching field. *Monitor on Psychology, 33*(4). Retrieved May 20, 2003, from http://www.apa.org/monitor/apr02/executive.html

Garman, A. N., Whiston, K. W., & Zlatoper, D. L. (2000). Graduate training and consulting psychology: A content analysis of doctoral-level programs. *Consulting Psychology Journal: Practice and Research, 50*(4), 207–217.

Glasser, J. K. (2002). Factors related to consultant credibility. *Consulting Psychology Journal: Practice and Research, 54*(1), 28–42.

Grodzki, L. (2002). *The new private practice.* New York: W. W. Norton.

Harcrow, A. (1998). Survey shows HR in transition. *Workforce, 77*(6), 73–79.

Harris, M. M. (2000). I-O psychology in the courtroom: Implications of the Daubert standard. *The Industrial-Organizational Psychologist, 38*(2). Retrieved May 20, 2003, from http://siop.org/tip/backissues/TipOct00/05Harris.htm

Hart, S. G. (2002). *A safe and secure system.* Retrieved June 5, 2002, from http://www.apa.org/ppo/issues/safesecure.paper.html

Hays-Thomas, R. L. (2000). The silent conversation: Talking about the master's degree. *Professional Psychology: Research and Practice, 31,* 339–345.

Herrman, D. (1997). Rewards of public service: Research psychologists in government. In R. J. Sternberg (Ed.), *Career paths in psychology: Where your degree can take you* (pp. 151–164). Washington, DC: American Psychological Association.

HR-Guide.com (2001). *Job Analysis: Overview.* Retrieved June 18, 2003, from http://www.hr-guide.com/data/G000.htm

Information Week (2002). *Salary advisor.* Retrieved June 16, 2002 at http://www.informationweek.com/advisor/salaryAdvisor

Joss, M. W. (2000). *The peak tech career: Project managers climb over each other for database gurus.* Retrieved May 20, 2003, from http://www.computeruser.com/articles/1904,5,16,1,0331,00.html

Kilburg, R. R. (1996). Toward a conceptual understanding and definition of executive coaching. *Consulting Psychology Journal: Practice and Research, 48,* 134–144.

Kuther, T. L. (2002). *Ethical conflicts in the teaching assignments of graduate students. Ethics and Behavior, 12,* 197–204.

Kuther, T. L. (2003a). *The psychology major's handbook.* Pacific Grove, CA: Wadsworth.

Kuther, T. L. (2003b). Teaching the teacher. Ethical issues in graduate student teaching. *College Student Journal, 37,* 219–224.

Lauber, J. K. (1997). An interesting career in psychology: Human factors psychologists in aviation. *Psychological Science Agenda.* Retrieved May 20, 2003, from http://www.apa.org/science/ic-lauber.html

Lloyd, M.A. (2000). *Master's- and doctoral-level careers in psychology and related areas.* Retrieved February 1, 2000, from http://www.psychwww.com/careers/masters.htm

Lloyd-Bostock, S. (1988). The benefits of legal psychology: Possibilities, practice and dilemmas. *British Journal of Psychology, 79,* 417–440.

Muchinsky, P. M. (2003). *Psychology applied to work.* Pacific Grove, CA : Wadsworth.

Murray , B. (2002). Psychologists help companies traverse the minefields of layoffs. *Monitor on Psychology.* Retrieved June 6, 2002, from http://www.apa.org/monitor/apr02/layoffs.html

Nielsen Norman Group. (2001). *Salary survey: User experience professionals, 2001.* Retrieved May 25, 2003, from http://www.nngroup.com/reports/salary/

Nietzel, M. T., & Dillehay, R. C. (1986). *Psychological consultation in the courtroom.* New York, NY: Pergamon Press.

Patterson, F. (2001). Developments in work psychology: Emerging issues and future trends. *Journal of Occupational and Organizational Psychology, 74,* 381–390.

Peters, R. L. (1992). *Getting what you came for: The smart student's guide to earning a master's or a Ph.D.* New York: Noonday Press.

Preparing Future Faculty (n.d.) *Preparing future faculty.* Retrieved January 18, 2002, from http://www.preparing-faculty.org/PFFWeb.Resources.htm

Reid, W. H. (1999). The top 19 things to remember when working with lawyers and courts. *Journal of Practical Psychology and Behavioral Health.* Retrieved August 15, 2002, from http://www.reidpsychiatry.com/columns/Reid07-99.pdf

Roediger, H. (1997). Teaching, research, and more: Psychologists in an academic career. In R. J. Sternberg (Ed.), *Career paths in psychology: Where your degree can take you* (pp. 7–30). Washington, DC: American Psychological Association.

Rosenstock, L. (1997). Work organization research at the National Institute for Occupational Safety and Health. *Journal of Occupational Health Psychology, 2*(1), 7–10.

Rotgers, F., & Barrett, D. (1996). Daubert v. Merrell Dow and expert testimony by clinical psychologists: Implications and recommendations for practice. *Professional Psychology: Research and Practice, 27,* 467–474.

Salary.com (2003). *Salary wizard.* Retrieved June 18, 2003, from http://www.salary.com

Salzinger, K. (1995). *The academic life. Psychological Science Agenda.* Retrieved on January 18, 2002, from http://www.apa.org/psa/janfeb95/acad.html

Scrader, B. (2001). Industrial/organizational psychology 2010: A research odyssey. In J. S. Halonen, & S. F. Davis (Eds.), *The many faces of psychological research in the 21st century.* Retrieved June 5, 2002, from http://teachpsych.lemoyne.edu/teachpsych/faces/text/Ch03.htm

Sebestyen, G. (2000). Watching the consultants. Science's Next Wave. Retrieved June 5, 2002, from http://nextwave.sciencemag.org/cgi/content/full/2000/07/26/1

Singleton, D., Tate, A., & Randall G. (2003). *Salaries in psychology: 2001: Report of the 2001 APA salary survey.* Retrieved November 8, 2003, from http://research.apa.org/01salary/salaries.pdf

Smith, L. (2002). Working extra hours pays off. *Information Week.* Retrieved June 16, 2002, from http://www.informationweek.com/story/IWK20020426S0002

Society for Human Resource Management, (n.d.) *Careers in human resource management.* Retrieved June 5, 2002, from http://www.shrm.org/students/careers.html

Society for Industrial and Organizational Psychology (1994). *Guidelines for education and training at the master's level in Industrial-organizational psychology.* Retrieved June 9, 2003, from http://siop.org/guidelines.htm

Society for Industrial and Organizational Psychology. (1999). *Guidelines for education and training at the doctoral level in industrial-organizational psychology.* Retrieved June 9, 2003, from http://siop.org/PhDGuidelines98.html

Somerville, K. (1998). Where is the business of business psychology headed? *Consulting Psychology Journal: Practice and Research, 50,* 237–241.

Tenopyr, M. L. (1997). Improving the workplace: Industrial/organizational psychology as a career. In R. Sternberg (Ed.), *Career paths in psychology: Where your degree can take you* (pp. 185–196). Washington, DC: American Psychological Association.

Traynor, W. J. & McKenzie, J. S. (1994). *Opportunities in human resource management careers.* Lincolnwood, IL: NTC Contemporary.

Tyler, R. R. (2000). An interesting career in psychology: Aviation human factors practitioner. *Psychological Science Agenda.* Retrieved May 25, 2003, from http://www.apa.org/science/ic-tyler.html

Usability Professionals Association. (2001). *2000 UPA member profile and salary survey.* Retrieved May 25, 2003, from http://upassoc.org/voice/survey/2000_survey.html

Vesilind, P. A. (2000). *So you want to be a professor? A handbook for graduate students.* Thousand Oaks, CA: Sage.

Vroom, V. H. (1997). Teaching the managers of tomorrow: Psychologists in business schools. In R. J. Sternberg (Ed.), *Career paths in psychology: Where your degree can take you* (pp. 49–70). Washington, DC: American Psychological Association.

Walker, L. E. (1990). Psychological assessment of sexually abused children for legal evaluation and expert witness testimony. *Professional Psychology: Research & Practice, 21*(5), 344–353.

Weiten, W. (2002). *Psychology: Themes and variations.* Pacific Grove, CA: Wadsworth.

Wetfeet.com. (2003). *Consulting.* Retrieved May 20, 2003, from http://www.wetfeet.com/asp/careerprofiles_comp.asp?careerpk=9

Williams, S., Wicherski, M., & Kohout, J. (1998). *Salaries in psychology: 1997.* Retrieved May 20, 2003, from http://research.apa.org/99salaries.html

Wiskoff, M. F. (1997). Defense of the nation: Military psychologists. In R. J. Sternberg (Ed.), *Career paths in psychology: Where your degree can take you* (pp. 245–268). Washington, DC: American Psychological Association.

Witherspoon, R., & White, R. P. (1996). Executive coaching: A continuum of roles. *Consulting Psychology Journal: Practice and Research, 48,* 124–133.

Wrightsman, L. S. (2001). *Forensic psychology.* Belmont, CA: Wadsworth.

Wrightsman, L. S., Greene, E., Neitzel, M. T., & Fortune, W. H. (2002). *Psychology and the legal system.* Belmont, CA: Wadsworth.

Wogalter, M. S., & Rogers, W. A. (1998). Human factors/ergonomics: Using psychology to make a better and safer world. *Eye on Psi Chi, 3*(1), 23–26.

Woods, D. (2002). *Behind human error: Human factors research to improve patient safety.* Retreived on November 8, 2003, from http://www.apa.org/ppo/issues/shumfactors2.html

Yund, M. A. (1998). Market research analyst, among other things. *Science's Next Wave.* Retrieved June 5, 2002, from http://nextwave.sciencemag.org/cgi/content/full/1998/06/04/8

Index